When Faith Meets Faith

WHEN FAITH
MEETS FAITH

by David M. Stowe

FRIENDSHIP PRESS   NEW YORK

LIBRARY OF CONGRESS CATALOG CARD NUMBER: 63-8691

Contents

Faith Meets Faith ✟ "It's only twenty meters deep. I'm going down. Want to come with me, François?" François did. This was cave country, the valley of the Ariège River, down near the Spanish border of France. Who could tell what Max and he might find? So Max Begouen and François Camel, French high school students, roped their way down the natural well they had located on that summer day in 1914. Jacques and Louis Begouen held the rope—and waited.

Half an hour went by. Three-quarters. Still no sound from the deep hole. Jacques and Louis looked at each other and decided they had better investigate. Just then happy shouts rang through the woods. Max and François were climbing back up the hill, their clothes muddy and torn. Their eyes were popping, and their faces wore big grins.

"It's a cave, with another opening down below. A big one. And covered with paintings! Animals, people, all mixed up. One tremendous guy with a huge reindeer mask and horns, presiding over the whole lot. They must be as old as the hills."

1 All Men Seek God

WORKS of art painted on southern European cave walls during the Ice Age offer a window by which we can look into the minds of our prehistoric ancestors. And there, across twenty centuries or more, we see two things: that ancient man was an artist, and that he was a religious being. The famous "sorcerer" of the Trois Frères cave, for example, is a mysterious figure who may either be a shaman of some prehistoric cult, or possibly a divine figure, a "reindeer god." Over all the magnificent, swarming vitality of animal life depicted in these paintings, there broods an unmistakable air of reverence and celebration. It is the mystical and supernatural potency of the living world that is being portrayed and worshiped.

Even earlier—perhaps one hundred thousand years ago—our Neanderthal forefathers were staining with red ocher the bodies and bones of their dead. Red is the color of life. Almost certainly Neanderthal men were trying to ensure continuing life after death for those they loved.

MAN, STILL THE RELIGIOUS BEING

We have not changed much in a thousand centuries. Highly complicated human beings in the second half of the twentieth century have the same irresistible drive to raise religious questions, to express themselves through religious practices, to belong to religious communities. Church members form a larger percentage of the American population in our day than in any year since 1620, when the Pilgrims landed with what was almost a captive congregation. Great literary artists wrestle with religious questions. Joyce, Kafka, Faulkner, Camus, Sartre, Becket—these men are labelled "atheist" or at least "agnostic"—yet Joyce wrote about the religious question of vocation in *Portrait of the Artist as a Young Man;* Camus dealt with *The Fall;* and Becket's *Waiting for Godot* seems to be about waiting for God.

This irrepressibly religious dimension of man's life comes out in the locker room as well as in the library. For example, the burly Baltimore Colts join in a prayer of thanksgiving after winning the world's professional football championship. Many a group of athletes has been known to do something similar.

In 1933 the then most powerful man in the world said: "I could destroy the Church in a few years. It is hollow and false and rotten through and through." But, when Hitler tried to beat it down, he found that the Christian faith had a staying power he could not match. Albert Einstein, the great Jewish scientist, also discovered that stamina:

8

Being a lover of freedom, when a revolution came in Germany I looked to the universities to defend it, knowing that they had always boasted of their devotion to the cause of truth; but, no, the universities immediately were silenced. Then I looked to the great editors of the newspapers whose flaming editorials in days gone by had proclaimed their love of freedom; but they, like the universities, were silenced in a few short weeks. . . . Only the Church stood squarely across the path of Hitler's campaign for supressing truth.[1]

"God is dead," said Nietzsche, the famous German philosopher, almost a hundred years ago. But the obituary was obviously premature. Man continues to be, as he began, an incurably religious being.

WHY IS MAN RELIGIOUS?

There have been many theories to account for man's stubborn concern with realities that cannot be touched or seen. One of the most famous of these starts from a feature of primitive religion called "totemism." Americans are familiar with the colorful totem poles carved out of huge cedar logs by the Indians of the Pacific Northwest. Various animals and birds provide the subject matter of such poles. These creatures are the "totems" of the clan or of the individual erecting the pole. They are believed to be blood relatives of the human group honoring them. They have mystical power and are thought in some sense to be divine.

Such ideas of kinship between a human group and certain animals provide the explanation of religion, some scholars have said. The totem is a symbol of the

[1] Notes will be found on p. 184.

9

group—the family or clan or tribe—that worships it. The real "god" is the group itself. The Eagle Clan expresses its own strength, its bravery, its glory, through the great bird that is its totem, just as his nation's flag symbolizes the object of a patriot's loyalty and devotion.

On this theory, religion is a way of honoring one's own group. The gods are creations of man's mind, symbols of his devotion to his family, his tribe, his nation, with its customs, its values, and its ambitions.

But if religion is just an expression of group loyalty ("an American's God is simply a glorified Uncle Sam"), why has it so often produced outstanding rebels against society? Buddha, Confucius, Amos, Jeremiah, Jesus, Muhammad, Luther, Gandhi—these are all men who fought against social customs and beliefs. A theory about religion that ignores its outstanding heroes can hardly satisfy us.

Another popular explanation of human religiousness was given by Sigmund Freud, founder of modern psychoanalysis. This was his line of thought:

Man is a very vulnerable and insecure creature. In primitive times he faced the threat of hunger and cold, of drought and hurricane, of fierce animals and poisonous plants. Many of these hostile forces of nature still worry him today. Moreover, there are all kinds of pressures from his fellow men. They threaten him with military aggression or with unfair business competition. Even in school it is a constant battle to keep ahead of assignments. And if you manage that, you are apt to be criticized as a grind.

So men invent a means of keeping their courage up. The little child, helpless and baffled by the big mysterious world, finds in his father a protector, a guide, a hero. The little man, tossed around by forces beyond his control, lost and lonely in a vast impersonal universe, creates for himself an imaginary heavenly Father. This Father-God becomes the object of his hero worship, his source of comfort and guidance. Religious beliefs are wish-fulfillments, and religion is an illusion. It may be helpful; it may bring comfort and a code to live by, but it comes out of our own heads and hearts. It does not refer to anything in the real world.[2]

Freud had something, of course. No one can look very long at the superstition and sentimentality that often go under the name of religion without admitting that wishing and dreaming have played their part. Yet the theory of religion as a comforting illusion breaks down when confronted with the facts. What did Jesus say? "Relax, follow me, and life will be easy and safe"? Hardly! "Sell all you have and give to the poor. If any man would come after me, let him take up his cross and follow me." The call of other great religious leaders, too, has been anything but comforting. They have challenged men to self-sacrifice, to heroic effort, to give up most of the easy and comfortable ways that we naturally prefer.

One more attempt to explain the universal power of religion in human life must be looked at. This is the official view of "the most dynamic force in the world today," Communism:

Some men, says Communist theory, have always exploited others. But, since keeping down their victims by force alone is difficult, they invent ideas to help them. Religion is the most important of these ideological means of exploitation. It tells the oppressed masses, "Be patient. Blessed are the meek and the poor. You suffer here, but you will have a happy life hereafter. God wants you to serve and obey your masters on this earth, and if you do, you will have a mansion in heaven." Thus religion is developed by rulers and their priests as an opiate for the people.

Again, one cannot simply dismiss this view. Too often religion has been allied with oppression. The great Frenchman Voltaire, who hated tyranny and was certainly no Communist, said he hoped to see the day when the last king was strangled with the entrails of the last priest!

And yet, religion has also been the most important source of human liberty. Hebrew prophets denounced economic oppression in words that are still the charter for social justice. Modern democracy was literally created by men who found their inspiration and guidance in religious faith: Cromwell, Penn, Hooker, Jefferson, Gladstone, Lincoln, Wilson. Take a map of the world. Mark on it the countries in which democratic liberties are most effective and secure. With almost no exceptions, these are countries having a strong tradition of free-church Christianity.

Actually, one can account for the power and prevalence of man's religious impulse only by seeing its roots deep in his essential nature. Man depends for his

12

very existence upon forces beyond his control. How can he help asking what kinds of forces these are, what they intend for him, why they made him as he is? He has a mind and a conscience, and he must make decisions. But what is right? And what will happen to the good that he feels compelled to serve? Will it simply disappear when he does, or is it somehow linked with the structure of the world itself? These inescapable questions are religious questions. By our very nature we are propelled into prayer, into worship, and theology—which means thinking seriously about God and the great questions of our nature, our destiny, and the universe in which he has placed us.

PANORAMA OF RELIGIOUS EXPRESSION

Unfortunately, religion is linked with the worst thinking as well as the best, with the grotesque as well as the sublime.

Look down a street in Bombay. Two men are coming. They are Jains, members of an Indian sect that takes very seriously the idea of kindness to all living creatures. They are carrying a light cot between them. The sheet looks curiously dirty. It is alive with bedbugs! Stopping before a Jain household, the men call out, "Who will feed the bugs?" If some pious member tosses a coin to them, one of the criers lies down very carefully on the bed and offers himself as a living feast to his fellow creatures. Thus the donor of the coin gains religious merit, the man on the cot a living—and the bedbugs a fine meal.[3]

Now step into a little Christian church on an island

13

in the central Pacific. Here missionaries landed more than a century ago. In spite of great difficulties, they communicated their faith; this church was built for the worship of God. Notice that the communion table is a large, curiously shaped rock. What is it? This rock was used in worship long before the church was built. From time immemorial it was the rock on which, each year, the head of a chosen youth was laid. Prayers and chanting invoked the attention of the god of fertility. Then with one blow of a heavy stone the youth's head was crushed, that prosperity might be ensured for another twelve months.

Human sacrifice, meals for bedbugs, prostitutes in temples, the persecution of unbelievers, the misery of the outcaste, holy wars—these too are part of the heritage of religion. No faith is free of such terrible things. Jesus was killed at the insistence of certain Jewish religious leaders. Followers of Jesus have murdered thousands of Jews in the centuries since. The Thirty Years' War that turned much of Europe into a graveyard and a desert, the Inquisition, the Salem witchcraft trials, Tennessee snakehandlers—such are some of the fruits of the "Christian religion."

This then is our problem. Everywhere we find man engaging in what he calls religion. Sometimes it seems to inspire and guide his highest achievements. Then we are shocked at the perversity and futility to which it leads him. What is the attitude of an intelligent Christian toward this amazing and baffling panorama? How does he judge other faiths than his own? What is the meaning of the vast diversity within Christianity itself? Has the Christian faith something unique and indispensible to offer those who have a different religious heritage?

To answer such questions, we must look more closely at some of the great religions by which our fellow men worship.

Faith Meets Faith ✝ Ray felt better already.
The murderous competition at the university now seemed
almost unreal. He breathed deeply, relaxing for the first
time in months.

The swami continued. "You see, self-knowledge sets
a person free. He comes to see that God is all, and that
he himself is one with God and with all things. True,
you will continue to work like an ordinary person, but
you will not be bound by the problems and results of your
work. Your spirit will always be at peace. Externals cannot disturb your true self, any more than rivers flowing
into the sea can disturb its depths."

"I suppose this means withdrawing from my church
and joining your center. Wonder what my folks will think
of that."

"Not at all," Ray's new friend replied. "We affirm the
value of all religions. Stay in your church. But understand Christianity in light of the deeper truth of Hindu
philosophy. All roads lead to God. We simply suggest
techniques by which your journey is hastened."[1]

Such tolerance impressed Ray, a sophomore to whom
the pressures of a great university had become overwhelming. From his Hindu missionary friend he heard a message that spoke to his need. He would return.

2 Hinduism

NO CHARACTERISTIC of the Hindu faith is more typical than hospitality to all forms of religious life. Hinduism is a container into which the ideas and experiences of the teeming Indian subcontinent have been pouring for five thousand years. (The word "Hindu" comes from the great river Indus, in what is now Pakistan, along which Indian civilization began about 3000 B.C.)

This, then, is Hinduism . . .

. . . A hump-backed bull shoulders his leisurely way through a crowded bazaar, demanding and receiving donations of food as his sacred right. (The same hump-backed bovine shape appears in cultic clay statuary of Mohenjo-daro, excavated recently after lying for four thousand years under the soil of the Indus valley.)[2]

. . . A quarter of a million people gather at a village near Indore to see a young widow cremate herself on her husband's funeral pyre in the ancient rite of suttee. They become disorderly when police intervene to stop this illegal act, and three people are killed in the ensuing riot.[3]

. . . Vinoba Bhave, clad like his master, Mahatma Gandhi, in a white loincloth, continues his walk of many thousands of miles across India, followed by adoring crowds and endowed with overwhelming spiritual authority. He asks those who have land to share it with those who have none. In this way he has been given more than four million acres for the poor.[4]

. . . Indian railways reap profits as millions of third-class passengers each year make their pilgrimages to sacred shrines. For many the holy Ganges River is the magnet. On a recent February day four million people came together to bathe at the junction of the Ganges and the Juma. Five hundred were crushed to death on the spot, but relatives consoled themselves with the thought that of all times and places to die, this was the best.[5]

. . . Dr. Sarvepalli Radhakrishnan delivers an inaugural lecture as Spalding Professor of Eastern Religions and Ethics before the University of Oxford: "Hinduism adopts a rationalist attitude in the matter of religion. It tries to study the facts of human life in a scientific spirit. . . . Religion is not so much a revelation to be attained by us in faith as an effort to unveil the deepest layers of man's being and get into enduring contact with them."[6]

. . . A rectangular stone four or five feet long drops from a cart onto an Indian street. A Christian removes it from the street as a traffic hazard, props it against a wall. Before it is removed, however, a little dab of betel juice drops on it. Someone, seeing the stone with a spot of red, supposes it to have spiritual properties and makes an offering of flowers and incense before it. Others follow her example. Then someone builds a platform under it as a base and erects a roof over it. A new Hindu shrine is born.[7]

SEVEN KEY IDEAS

Hinduism, then, is a family of religions. But as one soaks himself in its sights and sounds, certain key ideas emerge. They are expressed in many different ways, but they hang together with a subtle logic. Let us follow the thread of these ideas, marking our progress with seven knots in the string.

Dharma

The Indian word for religion is *dharma*. But *dharma* means something more like "duty" than like "religion" in our sense. Basic to a person's religious life is the performance of his duty. Note, however, that it is *his* duty. *Dharma* is not a set of general rules, like the Ten Commandments, but a varying prescription for each individual according to his age, family position, sex, education, and the like.

In the *Bhagavad-Gita,* most important of the Hindu scriptures, the god Vishnu appears to Arjuna the warrior, who is paralyzed by moral scruples. He shrinks from the suffering and death he is about to inflict. But Vishnu urges him to fight. As a member of the warrior caste, it is his duty. To leave the battle would be more than a disgrace; it would be a sin.[8]

Mahatma Gandhi, though a pacifist, endorsed this teaching. In favor of obedience to caste duty he wrote: "Why should we choose to claim as individuals the right during this present brief life-period to break through all the conventions wherein we were placed at birth by God Himself?"[9]

Samsara

Acceptance of an inferior or a distasteful *dharma* is made easier by a second fundamental Hindu idea. *Samsara* (reincarnation) is the belief that the soul is born and reborn over and over again, on different levels of existence. Just as the spirit that dwells in this body passes through childhood, youth, and old age, so at death it merely passes into another kind of body as a person might change clothes.

So then, Vishnu tells Arjuna, he need not be unduly concerned about those he will slay. Death is certain for the living; rebirth certain for the dead. His slaying makes no great difference.[10] Even Mahatma Gandhi defended the caste system on the same basis. Since any given lifetime is only one of a long series, don't let its troubles worry you. Accept it as a discipline suited to your soul's present stage of development. If it seems miserable, you will have other chances.[11]

This conviction that the soul endures through innumerable lives on earth, in varying forms of plant, animal, and human existence, is strange to most Americans. Yet it is the common belief of much of Asia. Along with it goes another conviction about the way these successive lives are linked together.

Karma

Karma is the word for that linkage. It means literally "action." Recall Newton's famous Third Law of Motion: "To every action there is an equal and opposite reaction." *Karma* is something like that, with the word "opposite" changed to "appropriate." Every action produces further action corresponding to it. Our actions in past lives have created the conditions under which we live now. Our present actions determine our future. By doing good today, we may be reborn tomorrow in a higher state, perhaps as a Brahman, a member of the highest caste. But thieving and lust will create a future life as a rat or a goat.

Atman

Lives come and go, strung like beads on the thread of *karma*. But in all this flux and change, there is something in every person that endures. "Worn-out bodies are shed by the Dweller within the body. New bodies are donned by the Dweller, like garments."[12] And here we come to a key idea of the Hindu way of thinking. Listen to the *Bhagavad-Gita*:

> Know this Atman
> Unborn, undying,
> Never ceasing,
> Never beginning,
> Deathless, birthless,
> Unchanging for ever.
> How can It die
> The Death of the body?

> Not wounded by weapons,
> Not burned by fire,
> Not dried by the wind,
> Not wetted by water:
> Such is the Atman,
> Not dried, not wetted,
> Not burned, not wounded,
> Innermost element
> Everywhere, always,
> Being of beings,
> Changeless, eternal,
> For ever and ever.[13]

Hindu religious architecture expresses this focus upon the *atman,* the inner soul. The holy of holies in a classic temple is a small dark room, a "wombhouse." It symbolizes the fact that the true object of worship is to be found in the dark and inmost recesses of the self.[14]

It is not too much to say, therefore, that the soul is the ultimate reality, equivalent to God. "Just as a jug dissolves into earth, a wave into water, or a bracelet into gold, even so the universe will dissolve into me. Wonderful am I! Adoration to myself! For when the world, from its highest god to its least stem of grass, dissolves, that destruction is not mine."[15]

The most famous expression of this conviction is found in an ancient scripture, the *Chandogya Upanishad.* "That which is the finest essence—this whole world has that as its Self. That is Reality. That is Atman. That art thou." Self and the Godhead, *atman* and *Brahman,* the soul of the individual and the Soul of the universe: these are really identical.

But notice that word "really." This identity of self and God is not seen on the surface of things. In fact, the whole set of habits, impulses, desires, ways of speaking and acting and thinking that make up our personality are *not* that Soul which is identical with Deity. The active personality that our friends know is an entirely different thing from the *atman*. More fundamental than the body is the mind, and below the mind is the subconscious, and then—far below that— the still, deep, eternal soul that is divine.

Maya

Hinduism has a word for the changing experience of the obvious and superficial "me," my "personality." The word is *maya,* which has the same root as our word "magic." The magician pulls a white rabbit out of his hat, but we don't take what we see at face value. Neither should we take too seriously the fact that we are born or die, we suffer or enjoy pleasure, we pass or flunk.

These events of everyday life—and of world history, too—are a kind of mirage. They are *lila,* the sport of the creator, the dance of the great god Siva. It is not quite true to say that they are utterly unreal. Even the magician is doing something. There would be no mirage if there were no desert and no sun. But they are not to be taken at face value. These experiences come and go—and nothing has really happened so far as reality—the *atman,* the self—is concerned. As with tricks done by a magician, what happens to people is just a kind of show.

Moksha

Now comes the "pay-off" word, *moksha. Moksha* means "release." It means being able to leave the theater when you have watched the show long enough.

That may not sound very important. But think of the best magician's act you have ever seen. You saw it once and loved it; you went back once, twice, perhaps three or four times. And you still enjoyed it. But suppose you have to sit in the theater and watch it over and over and over again. You get sleepy, you get bored—but the act goes on. The same old white rabbits, the same line of chatter, the same smile on the face of the same girl being sawed in two again. After a while the very thought of seeing it again is torture. But this is *samsara,* the literally endless cycle of the play of life. And you have only begun to watch! At this point your all-absorbing question becomes: How do I get out of this theater? (Dying won't do it, since death only leads to rebirth.)

Moksha stands for a blessed permanent exit from the cycle of rebirth. It is release from the intolerable dreariness of participation in the world of *maya,* the never-ending play of illusions in which nothing important ever really happens. *Moksha* is the goal of Hinduism, its term for salvation.

Since it must be completely different from anything that happens in the *maya* world of ordinary experience, *moksha* is difficult to describe. Probably the closest parallel is found in the experience of deep, dreamless sleep. "In this state a father is no father, a mother is no mother, the worlds are no worlds, the Vedas [scriptures] no Vedas. In this state a thief is no thief, the killer of a noble brahmin is no killer. . . . [This form of his] is untouched by good works and untouched by evil works."[16]

Yogas

How is the exit from the *maya* theater to be achieved? Through special techniques called *yogas*. *Yoga,* from the same root as "yoke," suggests the discipline that is required to break the chain of *karma,* the law that binds one to a never-ending series of rebirths.

There are a number of these disciplines of salvation suited to the varied conditions of life. For different temperaments different disciplines will be most congenial and most effective. Ultimately they all lead to the same goal. You choose the religious path most suitable for you.

So we find ourselves at the place where we began: the amazing tolerance and inclusiveness of Hinduism. There are many ways to God. Let us explore those most highly recommended by Hindu experience.

FOUR WAYS OF RELIGIOUS LIVING

The Yoga of Action

For active Americans, Hinduism has a *yoga* that is very appealing. Called *karma-yoga* ("action-discipline"), it prescribes a path to salvation through doing the right things. You follow your *dharma,* the code for your own particular life. But you do so in utter indifference to the results of your actions. Thus you become detached from the round of active life. The visible world ceases to concern you. You are spiritually free from its magic spell. So far as you are concerned, the show is over. And at that point you can leave the theater in peace.

This is easier to say than do, however. It is exceedingly hard to perform the strenuous and often distasteful duties of active life without putting your heart into your work. Yet when that happens you become involved, and you create "bad *karma*" which, rather than releasing you, ties you more firmly to *maya*. So the *Bhagavad-Gita* recommends more highly a second *yoga*, that of *bhakti*, which stresses loving devotion to one's divine Lord.

The Yoga of Devotion

Much of the great religious poetry of Hinduism derives from *bhakti*. Tulsi Sahib writes:

As the spider time and again runs upward with the gossamer thread,
Set thy face toward Him, O my heart!
Leave other masters, serve only Him who is thine like a faithful bride.
Thou canst see the Lord with the lamp of devotion alone, set on the salver of faith:
And *bhakti* more than learning will dispel the darkness of thy doubt, O my heart![17]

The greatest figure in modern Hinduism is Sri Ramakrishna Paramahamsa, who revived the power of *bhakti* devotion about a century ago. (His Ramakrishna Mission sent to America the swami with whom our chapter began.) He delighted in all kinds of religious intimacies with the divine. "I want to commune with God through various relationships," he said, "sometimes regarding myself as His servant, sometimes as His friend, sometimes as His mother, and sometimes as His sweetheart. I want to make merry with God. I want to sport with God."[18]

Rather daring language for religious devotion! But Hinduism is not afraid of passion. Words and images drawn from sexual love play a major part in the Hindu devotional tradition. In the scriptures called the *Puranas,* a key figure is the young god Krishna and his amorous exploits with the farmers' daughters of ancient India. Radha, the milkmaid who loves Krishna with total abandon, is a favorite symbol of the soul devoted to its Lord.[19] This erotic vein in Hinduism shows up in temple statuary, where sometimes the frankest scenes of love between man and woman are displayed.

But by now you will be wondering just who this God —or these gods—may be, to whom such devotion is desired. The world of Hinduism is full of deities. Some say there are 300 million of them. At the head of this swarming crowd are the Hindu trinity of gods: Brahma, the Creator; Vishnu, the Preserver (whom we have met in the *Bhagavad-Gita*), and Siva, the Destroyer (he is also the divine Dancer whose play creates the world). Most Hindus today are either Vaishnavites, devotees of Vishnu in one form or another, or Saivites, worshipers

27

of Siva. A third large group focuses its devotion on the great Mother-goddess Kali.

Vishnu says in the *Bhagavad-Gita,*

> In every age I come back
> To deliver the holy,
> To destroy the sin of the sinner,
> To establish righteousness.[20]

In other words, the great god incarnates himself over and over again: as animal, as man, as the god Krishna, and as the god Rama. (Some modern devotees add Buddha and Christ to this list of incarnations or avatars of Vishnu.) Likewise Siva appears in many forms, and Kali. But why are the gods so shifty?

The answer is basically simple. Ultimate Reality is One: the eternal Soul, *atman-Brahman.* But it is symbolized in an infinite number of ways, each appropriate to some aspect of the world of *maya*-existence and to the varying temperaments, needs, and interests of worshipers. Each such god-figure is really only a symbol, not a person. Such incarnations as Krishna and Rama are mythological figures, not at all comparable to the flesh-and-blood Jesus Christ of history. The world of the gods is *maya* just as much as the world of man.

The Yoga of Knowledge

The third approach to the religious life is that of *jnana,* which is knowledge or understanding. The truly thoughtful religious person strives to realize that nothing really matters except the impersonal, formless, eternally unchanged and unchanging One. He heeds the words of the ancient teacher:

"That which is beyond caste and creed, family and lineage, which is devoid of name and form, merit and demerit, that which transcends space, time, and sense-objects, that Brahman art thou. Meditate on this in thy mind.

"That which is free from birth, growth, maturity, decline, infirmity, and death; that which is indestructible; that which is the cause of the projection, maintenance, and dissolution of the universe—that Brahman art thou. Meditate on this in thy mind."[21]

The Yoga of Spiritual Exercise

A purely intellectual understanding of these things is hardly enough, however. Therefore, Hinduism offers a fourth yoga, a practical discipline for filling one's whole being with the consciousness of *atman-Brahman* and freeing one from all attachment to the world of things. This is called *rajayoga.*

The aim of *rajayoga* is to quiet the mind so completely and focus it so sharply that nothing whatever can disturb its meditation on *atman-Brahman.* The yogi sits cross-legged in deep contemplation. He learns to control his breath (after long and patient practice he may be able to remain buried alive for several days!). Then he gets control of his restless thoughts and slows or even stops the stream of consciousness. At a higher level he concentrates his awareness on just one part of the body—perhaps his navel or the tip of his nose. Finally, he rejects the outer aspects of this object and contemplates only its essence. He is aware of no navel or nose, but only navelness or noseness, and finally only "isness." This is called *samadhi* or total absorption. Seeing a yogi in this condition, we might say he is in a trance. He would call it isolation or desirelessness. He is completely cut off from the flow of normal sensations and events. He has attained release from *maya*.[22]

There is a very interesting variation on these traditional *yogas*, called *tantra*. Instead of drawing away from the world of everyday objects and events, *tantra* seeks to realize the fundamental unity of all things by experiencing them to the full. Sri Ramakrishna, the modern Hindu saint, followed the way of tantrism. His followers report: "Evil ceased to exist for him, and the word *carnal* lost all meaning. He went into ecstacy at the sight of a prostitute, of drunkards reveling in a tavern, and of sexual union of a dog and a bitch. The whole world was revealed to him as the play of Siva-Sakti, and he beheld everywhere the power and beauty of the Divine Mother."[23]

These terms, "Siva-Sakti" and "Divine Mother," require closer attention. Siva is the divine Dancer, and Sakti is his counterpart in female form. Siva is identified with the passive, eternal Brahman; Sakti is his "energy," exciting him to creation. It is the interplay of Siva and Sakti that creates the world. The embrace of these two is a common motif in Oriental religious art.

By natural extension Sakti is identified with the entire life-bearing female element in nature, and with the figure of a Mother-Goddess that comes down from the Indus Valley cult of 3000 B.C. This Divine Mother has a large group of devotees, who worship her under such names as Kali, Durga, and Parvati. Since creation inevitably leads to destruction, Kali is often pictured with blood dripping from her mouth, wearing a necklace of skulls, holding a severed head in one hand, and trampling on the corpse of her consort, Siva. She is goddess of epidemics and earthquakes, floods and storms. Animals are slain in her temples. Before the Indian Government wiped it out, a sect of Kali devotees called *thugin* (source of our word "thug") went around the countryside strangling human victims to satisfy her thirst for human blood.[24]

Thoughtful Hindus explain their worship of Kali by saying that the tragic and terrible aspects of experience are as much a part of *atman-Brahman,* the One Reality, as the good and the pleasant.

TOWARD AN EVALUATION

How shall we, as outsiders, take stock of this vast and fascinating panorama of religion called Hinduism? Christians—and Westerners in general—are accustomed to judging the value of religion by its ethical results. Jesus indicated the validity of this approach when he said, "By their fruits you shall know them." Let us look first, then, at the moral emphases that are part of Hinduism.

Hindu Ethics

Great modern Hindus such as Gandhi, Bhave, and Ramakrishna have certainly given outstanding moral leadership. Gandhi's rules for his ashram or community of disciples provide an interesting summary of Hindu ethics. They include the following:

. . . A VOW OF TRUTH

This is an absolute claim, not simply, "Honesty is the best policy." Central to truth as Gandhi understood it is *ahimsa*, which literally means noninjury. Gandhi believed firmly that *ahimsa* represents tremendous force. He called it *satyagraha*, literally "power of truth," and depended upon this moral power of nonviolent goodwill for practical social reform. The winning of Indian independence from Britain is usually credited to this strategy of Gandhi's. Likewise Bhave depends upon *satyagraha* for the success of his land-gift movement whereby he seeks a just reapportionment of land holdings in India.

. . . A VOW OF CELIBACY

All physical desire must be renounced, even in marriage. Relationships should be purely spiritual.

. . . A VOW OF CONTROL OF APPETITE

All stimulating and exciting seasonings that do not add to food value but simply please the appetite are a hindrance to ethical living. Even animals eat only for nourishment, not fleshly enjoyment. The human gourmet is indeed a poor creature.

. . . A VOW OF NONTHIEVING

This is very broadly interpreted to mean living on a bare subsistence level, using nothing that is not essential. "If I take anything that I do not need for my own immediate use and keep it," Gandhi said, "I steal it from somebody else."

. . . A VOW OF NONPOSSESSION

This means giving away all one's surplus until the standards of the poorest have been raised.

. . . A VOW OF SWADESHI OR "BUY AT HOME"

Gandhi felt that we depart from a sacred law of our being when we leave our own neighborhood and go elsewhere to satisfy our wants. In other words, each person and each group should be self-sustaining and continue in an accustomed way of life. It is wrong to seek artificial luxury through widespread trade and a cosmopolitan culture.

. . . A VOW OF FEARLESSNESS

"There is only One whom we have to fear, that is God."

. . . A VOW AGAINST UNTOUCHABILITY

Although Gandhi defended the caste system, he fought against the degrading of outcastes. He denied that they carry a ritual pollution that makes them "untouchable."

. . . A VOW OF KHADDAR OR LABOR

Every Gandhian was expected to do some manual work daily to testify to the dignity of labor. Hence the famous spinning wheel with which the Mahatma was often photographed.[25]

Most items on this list quite clearly belong to the Hindu heritage. Others, however, come from elsewhere. The concern with social reform, the interpretation of *ahimsa* in a positive sense as universal love, the affirmation of human dignity in the outcaste and in labor, the "fear of God" that brings fearlessness toward men—these are not part of the classical Hindu outlook. They come rather from the West with its Christian social tradition.

Hinduism Today and Tomorrow

A final question might be: Is present-day Hinduism the same as the religion we have been examining? Certainly Hinduism is changing. How could it be otherwise with a faith that has for thousands of years been incorporating new ideas and practices into its life, with discrimination toward none and with toleration toward all? Modern ideas are crowding into Hinduism today. No doubt they will continue to do so.

It is the encounter with Christianity that has generated much of this impulse to change. The founder of Brahmo Samaj, a Hindu sect organized in 1830, was a devotee of Christ. "The mighty artillery of His love He levelled against me," said this Hindu leader, "and I was vanquished and fell at His feet."[26] And a recent book on education published by the Government of India begins by quoting Jesus: " 'I came not to destroy but to fulfill,' said the Great Messiah. That is the spirit with which we should be inspired in these times."[27] It was the New Testament that confirmed Gandhi's belief in nonviolent resistance. He wrote, "When I read in the Sermon on the Mount such passages as . . . 'Love your enemies; pray for them that persecute you, that ye may be sons of your Father which is in heaven,' I was simply overjoyed."[28]

One of the most important questions of our century is this: What will happen in the continuing encounter between Hinduism and Christianity? Will—and can —Hinduism so fundamentally adjust its approach to life that it may support real progress? Will Hinduism succeed in swallowing up Christianity in India and making it just one more caste and one more *yoga*? Or will the Christian church and the Christian message become a strong, independent, and vital force in this age-old land of religious seeking?

Faith Meets Faith ✟

Mr. Stewart's enthusiasm impressed Elizabeth. He was the most popular teacher in school, with a really sharp mind.

"Actually, Liz, there is no way to express what a difference Zen training has made in my life. It's like getting out of jail after a long sentence, or like hearing that somebody has just left you a million dollars! The whole world feels different, like the magic day when suddenly, after a long hard winter, you know that spring is here."

Mr. Stewart stopped, then smiled at his favorite student. "I'm afraid I get carried away. But, really, this has made me a better man. It's even made me a better Christian, because it helps me make sense out of such ideas as the Trinity, the Incarnation, and the Resurrection."

Elizabeth was fascinated. She had come to see Mr. Stewart for advice on a paper she was writing on "Buddhism as a Cultural Influence in the Far East." But all those strange terms—*Mahayana, bodhisattva, nirvana, karma*—what did they mean? She was delighted to find that her teacher knew so much about Buddhism. Now she began to think that this study might help her with some of her own religious doubts. The standard answers she heard on Sunday morning did not entirely convince her. And so she opened her notebook as Mr. Stewart started to talk again.[1]

3 Buddhism

DISCOVERING Zen Buddhists in America is no longer surprising. This colorful sect has evoked articles in *Time* and *Playboy* as well as in *The Christian Century*. Kerouac's novel, *The Dharma Bums,* reflects the great influence Zen has had on the "beat" generation.

Actually, Zen is not the largest sect of Buddhism in North America. The Buddhist Churches of America belong to the Jodo-Shin sect. Both Zen and Jodo-Shin, in turn, are sects of that great branch of Buddhism called Mahayana, prominent all over northern Asia. Another great branch flourishes under the label Hinayana. Yet all these, and scores of other Buddhist groups, have a common origin in that very remarkable man who lived about six centuries before Christ and whom the world has known as Gautama the Buddha.

GAUTAMA BUDDHA AND JESUS CHRIST

Of all the human beings who ever lived, Buddha is probably the one most like Jesus of Nazareth in his influence upon history. Gautama was born not in a

37

stable but in a palace, near the border between present-day northern India and Nepal. His father surrounded him with sensual pleasures and material comforts in order to insulate him from the sorrows, frustrations, and pains of mankind.

In his twenties, however, Prince Gautama did discover these bitter realities. Legend tells of his accidental meetings with a senile man, a desperately sick man lying in his own filth, and a corpse being carried to the funeral pyre. Thus, he learned that the vigor and enjoyments of the body last only a few years; that even in those years man is subject to pain and disease; and that at the end death comes to everyone. Brooding on these discoveries, he encountered a Sadhu, a Hindu holy man. From him he learned that it is possible to leave the futile world of sensual desires and enjoyments and to seek an abiding peace and satisfaction. That night he kissed his infant son and his sleeping wife goodby and went out to seek that peace.

For seven years his search took the forms traditional in Hinduism of that time and place. He practiced *yoga* and speculated philosophically on the cosmos, the One, and the soul. When that got him nowhere, he almost starved himself until, "when I thought I would touch the skin of my stomach, I actually took hold of my spine!" But it was all in vain, for no transforming insight came.

Then he remembered a happy experience of his youth. "I was seated under the cool shade of a rose-apple tree, and without sensual desires, without evil ideas, I attained and abode in the first trance of joy and pleasure arising from seclusion and combined with reasoning and investigation. Perhaps this is the way to Enlightenment," he thought.[2] And so there arose his great idea of the Middle Way, avoiding both self-indulgence and self-punishment, and making full use of careful thought without tumbling into an abyss of mystical speculation.

Having gotten his sense of direction, Gautama seated himself under a spreading tree near Gaya in northeastern India and began a long period of concentrated meditation (forty-nine days, the legend says). Though tempted by demons, he maintained his vigilance and resolution. Finally, at the full moon of May, 544 B.C. (the traditional date; probably about 540 B.C. in reality) he entered into a vivid experience of "enlightenment" (*bodhi*). Henceforth, Gautama was to be called "Buddha," the Enlightened One. An ancient account describes the experience: "My mind was emancipated from the canker of sexual desire, from the canker of desire for existence and from the canker of ignorance. And in me emancipated there arose the knowledge of my emancipation. I realized that destroyed is rebirth, the religious life has been led, what was to be done is done, there is nothing for me beyond this world."[3]

The Buddha then made his way to the holy city of Benares on the Ganges, and there preached his first sermon to five former companions of his ascetic period. For the next forty-five years, he traveled up and down northern India, preaching and gathering disciples. Finally, after accidentally eating a dish containing poisonous mushrooms, he called his disciples around him and took his leave of life with the final words: "Work out your salvation with diligence."

As a result of this long ministry, ended only in his eightieth year, Gautama left behind a well-organized and extensive fellowship of monks and a smaller group of nuns dedicated to the search for enlightenment. This order became one of the Three Jewels of Buddhism, the *sangha* (order) which is the visible community of the faith. The other jewels are the Buddha himself, and the *dharma* (the teaching or law).

BUDDHIST TEACHING

For anyone familiar with Hinduism, Buddhist *dharma* will hold few surprises. Here are the key Hindu concepts that Gautama Buddha never called into question.

Hindu Elements Accepted

. . . SAMSARA

This is the endless round of rebirths that makes life and its difficulties so hard to bear.

. . . KARMA

Karma points to the momentum of actions in one life that carries over into the next, determining its circumstances according to the merits or demerits that have been accumulated.

. . . MAYA

In Buddhism as in Hinduism, *maya* is the "magic" or the illusory quality of the world of everyday experience.

40

. . . MOKSHA

Buddhism never questioned the desirability of release from the pressure of this illusory, everyday existence and from the endless cycles of rebirth into painful new lives.

. . . YOGA

All Buddhist sects have adopted *yoga*, the disciplines by which release may be achieved. These involve not only control of the body and mind and devotion to truth, but understanding by which one "sees through" illusions.

Hindu Elements Rejected

Gautama sharply rejected, however, three other aspects of Hindu thought and practice:

. . . SCRIPTURAL AND PRIESTLY AUTHORITY

One strand in Hinduism has always emphasized the ancient Vedic scriptures and their priestly ritual and sacrifice. Gautama swept all this aside, saying that each person must achieve salvation by his own thinking and his own right action.

. . . CASTE

Gautama completely rejected the Hindu way of grading people according to the caste into which they were born. He took the word *dharma*, meaning "duty" or "way of life," which Hinduism had made the basis of caste distinctions, and gave it a very different meaning. *Dharma* for Buddhism became the Teaching, the Way by which *all* persons ought to organize their lives. Understanding this "natural law" of one's personality and of the world around us is the way to happiness, serenity, and finally salvation.

. . . ATMAN-BRAHMAN

Hinduism had a central pivot on which the whole system turned: the identity of the inmost soul (*atman*) with the eternal, infinite and absolute One (*Brahman*), which is the inmost Soul of the universe. Gautama dismissed both of these at one fell swoop, leaving nothing but—what?

Here is Buddhism's most baffling question. Certainly, Gautama himself wanted to sidestep endless disputes about the soul and God. His concern was purely practical. To one of his disciples who persisted in asking about the eternal Brahman, he rejoined that, whether or not he believed in Brahman, "There still remain birth, old age, death, sorrow, lamentation, misery, grief and despair, for the extinction of which in the present life I am prescribing."[4] Then he told a parable:

A man was wounded by an arrow thickly smeared with poison. In desperation his friends and relatives hurried to find a physician to remove the arrow and to treat him for the poison. But the wounded man said, "Wait! I can't have this physician touch me until I find out what caste he belongs to. And I must know his name and his family background. And where does he come from? Is he tall, short or middle-sized?" That man died before he ever learned the answers to his questions![5]

Gautama, reacting against the complexities of Hinduism, kept his message simple. He summarized it in Four Noble Truths.

42

Buddha's Noble Truths

. . . PAIN

"Birth is painful, old age is painful, sickness is painful, death is painful, sorrow, lamentation, dejection, and despair are painful. Contact with unpleasant things is painful, not getting what one wishes is painful."[6]

. . . THE CAUSE OF PAIN

The cause of pain is "craving, which tends to rebirth [by creating *karma*] . . . the craving for passion, the craving for existence, the craving for nonexistence."

. . . THE CESSATION OF PAIN

Pain ceases with the absolute end of craving.

. . . THE WAY THAT LEADS TO CESSATION OF PAIN

One achieves freedom from all craving by following the noble Eightfold Path:

1. *Right Views.* First of all comes a correct understanding of our problem, which understanding is expressed in the first three Noble Truths. It is necessary also to understand the nonreality of the self that undergoes all this suffering.

2. *Right Intention.* Correct understanding must not remain a merely theoretical or abstract thing. It must be translated into will, into an energetic striving to act upon truth.

3. *Right Speech.* Words must correspond with our inner attitudes. The things we say have a great in-

fluence not only on others but on our own quality of life.

4. *Right Action.* The Five Precepts spell out the meaning of right action. These correspond in a sense to the Ten Commandments.[7]

> Do not kill (extended to the whole realm of living things as far as possible. This is the traditional Indian *ahimsa* in its fuller meaning of noninjury and goodwill toward all fellow beings.)
> Do not steal.
> Do not commit any impurity.
> Do not lie.
> Do not use intoxicants.

5. *Right Livelihood.* Obviously, you should not allow yourself to be drawn into an occupation—such as butchering, soldiering, or bartending—that would lead you into wrong action. The Buddhist ideal is the life of a monk or a nun, for only in the monastery can one fully practice nonattachment to all persons and total renunciation of all desires. True, the lay person also has a respected place. But he probably has to wait for another life, in which he becomes a monk, before he can hope for salvation.

6. *Right Effort.* One has to "abide vigilant, strenuous, and resolute," in Gautama's words, to make progress. Evil thoughts are to be overcome, passions controlled. Right thoughts must be pursued with vigor.

7. *Right Mindfulness or Alertness.* By this Gautama meant primarily a habit of constant, cool, objective analysis of the real situation. For example, if you are plagued with desire for bodily pleasures, go

out to the field where the corpses are burned. As you look at the half-burned bodies and the disjointed bones, you can contemplate the body "as it really is," in life and in death. This beautiful girl who stirs me so—what is she really but a bag of skin filled with a pulp of blood, tissue, and repulsive internal organs hung on a grisly skeleton? And this body of mine, which I cherish and pamper—what is it but the same thing, destined for disease, decay, and death? Why do I value it so? Why do I even insist that it is "mine"? It is just another body, taking its short and ignoble journey between birth and death, one insignificant swirl of matter in a world full of pain and illusion. Let it go!

8. *Right Concentration.* The crown of religious life is such absolute control of the mind that it remains completely focused upon truth. All things of time and space and sense drift away; all feelings and desires are stilled. One is united with ultimate reality, liberated from craving, from the power of suffering, from *karma* and rebirth. He is an *arahat,* ready for Buddhahood and for nirvana.

THE BUDDHIST GOAL

Nirvana corresponds to heaven in the Christian view of salvation but is even more difficult to describe. It originates in a negative idea: the absence of all that is unpleasant, raised to an infinite degree! Nirvana, an Indian word, literally means "blowing out," as a candle flame is extinguished by a breath. So when all the fires of passion and desire, of anxiety and striving and pain, are blown away, when the candle of life is put out never to be rekindled in rebirth, then one is in nirvana. He is, literally, "extinguished."

Yet Buddhists have generally denied that the goal of religious life is simply nothingness. "In [the scriptures] it is defined as: Highest Refuge, Safety, Unique, Absolute Purity, Supramundane Security, Emancipation, Peace, and the like. It is a blowing out of man's desires, and that blowing out of desire leaves a man free. . . . Freedom means that one cannot be made a slave to anyone or anything because one is free from personal desire, free from resentment, anger, pride, fear, impatience—free from all craving."[8]

Buddhist art helps where words fail (and that words do fail is a basic Buddhist conviction). In the famous Ajanta Caves in central India is a gigantic statue of the Buddha carved from the solid rock but still embedded in it and surrounded by it. He is lying on his side, completely at rest. His eyes are closed, and there is an expression of absolute repose on the great face. There is neither joy nor pain here, neither consciousness nor death, but only the suggestion of total peace in having returned to the one and timeless reality underlying the world of time and change.[9]

TOWARD AN EVALUATION

Such is the gospel of Gautama the Buddha. His practical spirit brought a welcome change from the jungle growth of Indian theological speculations. His preaching and his example constantly stressed sane moderation of thought and behavior. His message was a realistic attempt to deal with the sadness of a world in which flowers wither and death separates those who love.[10]

As an American philosopher has said, "always and everywhere, when men begin to reflect, their reaction towards a world seen without God and without purpose is dark with despair and bitter with resentment."[11] But this is precisely the view of things that Gautama did accept, and made the basis of his gospel! He offered no illusions, only a clear, reasonable analysis of experience and a sane, wholesome way of life. He called upon men to think for themselves and to test in their own lives the possibility of living by what he had found to be true.

Gautama's special contribution to man's religious life surely includes his own personality. He was a truly great and beloved human being, an almost unique combination of a cool scientific head with the devoted sympathy of a warm and loving heart. His devoted pity for every kind of suffering life was endless, yet he was never blinded by sentiment. His views were radically democratic even though he himself was an aristocrat. He was an accomplished diner-out, with a store of anecdotes and a real sense of humor, the perfect guest. Someone has called him a combination of St. Francis and Socrates!

Southern Buddhism

In several southern Asian countries, Buddhism is so dominant that recent revivals of nationalism in Ceylon, Burma, and Thailand have involved impressive Buddhist revivals also. In Burma, Buddhism has officially been declared the state religion. Almost every Thai man is a Buddhist monk for at least a short period. This south Asian Buddhism is commonly called *Hinayana* ("Little Vehicle") but the less derogatory term *Therevada,* the "Religion of the Elders," is preferred. It claims to be closer to Gautama's teaching and to primitive Buddhism than the northern Buddhism, which dubbed itself *Mahayana* ("Greater Vehicle"). Certainly, the scriptures of *Hinayana* represent the earlier strands of Buddhist tradition. There is a strong emphasis on monasticism and a preference for practice of religion rather then philosophizing about it.

Most basic, perhaps, is a continuation of Gautama's emphasis on salvation by one's own efforts:

"By one's self the evil is done; by one's self one suffers; by one's self evil is left undone; by one's self one is purified. The pure and the impure stand and fall by themselves; no one can purify another."[12]

Among well-educated southern Buddhists, Gautama's agnosticism and humanism persist. To them devotional practices are simply exercises in spiritual self-cultivation. One monk, replying to a visitor who asked to whom he was praying and for what, said, "I am praying to nobody, and praying for nothing." Images and relics of the Buddha—a tooth, a footprint, a hair, and the like—are interpreted by Buddhist leaders as merely means by which the mind is inspired to think and feel like the Buddha himself.[13]

But for the average southern Buddhist, devotion to such images and relics is certainly more than a calculated mental exercise. To him Buddha is a divine being resident in heaven. Prayer to him has an effect, both on this life and on the life to come.

While southern Buddhism has been faithful to the practical and rational emphasis in Gautama's teaching, it may have neglected his essential spirit. He talked about calculated self-cultivation but exhibited an outgoing, self-giving spirit. This became the ideal that dominated Buddhism as it went north.

Northern Buddhism

Mahayana, or northern Buddhism, offers a hospitable way to salvation for all men, whether or not they are capable of the spiritual feats of the Buddha himself. It also represents a protest against certain difficulties in original Buddhism. For example, Gautama's ban on theological and philosophical speculation really amounted to saying, "I don't know" to all the great questions about the world, the soul, and God that men have asked from the beginning of time. Again, his apparent denial of a true self runs counter to our own experience of personal existence. What is more, how is rebirth possible with nothing to be reborn? Gautama's unconcern about God also denied man's hunger for the divine. The idea that only a few monks could achieve salvation broke down before the hunger of all men for fulfillment.

And so, Mahayana arose in China, Tibet, Korea, and Japan. It expressed, through scores of sects, five emphases: a systematic philosophy and theology, divine beings to worship, an immortal soul to save, a religious path fully open to lay people as well as to monks, and saviors whom ordinary men could love and trust for salvation.

Perhaps the profoundest contribution of the Mahayana spirit is the *bodhisattva,* a savior. For southern Buddhism the supreme figure is the *arahat,* he who has followed the Eightfold Path to the top of the mountain and achieved enlightenment. But what if the *arahat,* having achieved salvation for himself, should then of his own free will refuse nirvana and turn back into the world of suffering and rebirth in order to help others? Doing so he becomes a *bodhisattva,* "one whose being is enlightenment," a compassionate savior. Along with this idea it was, of course, necessary to modify the original concept that everyone strictly works out his own salvation. The goodness of the *bodhisattva* becomes available to the needy.[14]

These savior-figures are not historical persons. Sakyamuni Gautama, the historic Buddha, plays very little part in Mahayana devotion. Rather, the great *bodhisattvas* are created by imagination, sometimes by adopting and modifying earlier gods. Kuan Yin, the lovely mother-figure who is often called Goddess of Mercy, was originally a male Indian deity! In such gracious saviors the Christian glimpses a spirit that may remind him of his own Master. Basically, however, the *bodhisattva* belongs to a religious world radically different from that of the Christian Savior. Even Mahayana Buddhism rest upon detachment from the illusions of existence. There is no ultimate difference between good and evil; nor is there any emphasis upon human sinfulness. There is bad *karma,* which produces misery, but that is really part of an impersonal cosmic order from which one should seek to become disengaged.

Salvation and Sympathy

Buddhist moral teaching springs from the conviction that, until we achieve salvation, we are bound up with all other living things in the beautiful but painful process of "existence." Out of this arises sympathy for our fellow creatures, a compassion like that so finely exemplified by Gautama. Moreover, the rule of *karma* ordains that good comes only from good. "Hatred does not cease by hatred at any time; hatred ceases by love."[15] To that law, that love, that *dharma*, the Buddhist is asked to give cheerful allegiance.

Faith Meets Faith ✠ Ginny had been enjoying the evening very much. The University Christian Center was having a joint program with the Young Muslim League. Two dozen students from the Middle East and Pakistan, all talking of a tour to Mecca, were on hand.

"Can Christians visit Mecca?" someone asked.

The Muslim League adviser, a visiting professor of medicine, was on his feet in a moment. "At present no non-Muslim can make this trip," he began. "But this situation may soon be changed. It's not a religious question at all, but political. Arabia is a backward country, suspicious of foreigners; its leaders don't want foreigners to see the disease and the dirt and the slavery.

"There is no religious reason whatever why Christians and Jews should not visit the holy places of Islam. After all, we all believe in the same God, we all have Scriptures with much in common, we all give honor to Abraham and Moses, and we all recognize Jesus as a great prophet. We belong to one great family of faiths."

Then discussion began in earnest. As Ginny listened, she wondered if the adviser was really right. Is there a special bond between Christian and Muslim and Jew? If so, what does it mean? It looked as if that evening might turn out to be very important for her understanding of what can happen when faith meets faith.

4 Watershed of Religions

IN OUR journey among the religions of our fellow men we come now to a watershed, where the streams of faith divide sharply and run toward different destinations.

THE ORIENTAL STREAM

We have seen some spectacular religious scenery in India and the Far East, all with a certain basic similarity. Hinduism and Buddhism, with all their immense variety, clearly belong to one great stream. Or, to change the figure, they belong to the same family of Oriental religions. Most of their fundamental ideas are the same. They see ultimate reality as basically impersonal. Salvation is escape from the frustrations of individual existence into unity with a vast, formless One, an infinite, shoreless, waveless ocean into which individual existence finally merges "as a dewdrop slips into the shining sea."

Even a brief encounter with other Eastern religions also reveals resemblances. Consider the fascinating

Chinese puzzle called Taoism (pronounced dow-ism). It centers in the idea of the Tao, the "Way" or "Law" or "Essence" of the universe, most commonly symbolized by the familiar *yin* and *yang*. The two "tadpoles" chasing each other within the circle show the interplay of cosmic forces. Man's salvation lies in merging his way of life with this quiet, beautiful, and inexorable Way. Religion means yielding to the power of the Tao by opening one's heart and mind to the mystic depth of mountains, sky, and river. (Historically the term Taoism has designated two other kinds of religion in addition to this profound and mystical philosophy of nature. It has meant a system of magic and superstition, purporting to tap the power of the Tao for private purposes; and also a system of mystical practices similar to Indian *rajayoga*, believed to bring identification with the Tao and consequent supernatural powers.)

In Japan the original religious tradition is called Shinto. It is perhaps the outstanding example of primitive nature religion surviving in a modern society. This folk religion keeps men in touch with the deities that inhabit the Japanese landscape. It is also a way of celebrating the unique place of the Japanese people in the universe. Its ancient myths describe the creation of the Japanese from the coupling of primeval nature gods and the descent of the Japanese imperial family from the sun goddess Ameratsu.

Divinities of all shapes and sizes swarm in the world of Shinto. There are fox spirits and the spirits of rocks and groves; Mt. Fuji and the spirits of Japanese war dead; father-sky and mother-earth. This is similar to the nature religion of ancient India, still reflected in village Hinduism and the swarming Hindu pantheon.

Confucianism, the other great spiritual force in Far Eastern life, stands somewhat apart from the mainstream of Oriental religion. Along with Buddha, Confucius towers over other religious figures of the East. Living at about the same time as the great Indian, this man who gave Chinese civilization its character is in some ways strikingly like Gautama. He, too, was a reformer of the stagnant religious and social order of his day. His spirit, too, was practical and down to earth. Confucius' emphasis was on man himself, his powers and his responsibilities. He said little about God, though he did call upon men to order their lives in accord with the structure (Tao) of the universe. Essentially man must save himself.

In sharp contrast to the Buddha, however, Confucius believed strongly that men can create a satisfying life on earth, within a just, harmonious, and beneficent social order. His prescription for the right ordering of the basic human relationships (father and son, elder and younger brother, husband and wife, older and younger friend, ruler and subject) was a blueprint for Chinese civilization, one of the most successful and durable communities in all history. In describing the individual qualities upon which that social order rests, he has sketched a splendid ideal of human excellence. It is an ideal of self-discipline, public spirit, moderation, intellectual vigor, and love of the arts. Sympathy is combined with absolute integrity and a keen sense of justice. According to the famous Confucian "silver rule," we are not to do to others what we would not have them do to us.

Critics of Confucius found the *chun-tzu*, the ideal Confucian gentleman, just a bit too worldly, however. One of them told this parable:

"Have you ever heard of the lice that live in trousers? The louse takes sanctuary in the depths of the seams, and . . . when it takes a walk, it carefully keeps to the edge of the seam. When it moves about, it never ventures beyond the confines of the seat and believes it is behaving with proper etiquette. When it is hungry it feeds on flesh, and is confident it can never starve. But when the trousers are taken to be boiled and pressed, the towns and cities of lice are destroyed. . . .

"Is not your 'perfect gentleman' who confines himself to the visible world like the lice who would live forever in the trousers?"[1]

So it was that Confucianism provided the model for the Chinese way of life and, in part, for Japan and Korea, too. But it was Buddhism, along with Taoism, that provided for China its element of mysticism, a sense of something beyond this life and a hope beyond the grave.

There is, however, one ingredient missing in all these varied and impressive recipes for living. It is God! There are, in the Oriental religions, all kinds of spirits and supernatural beings. There is also a concept of Ultimate Reality.

But for one living and personal God, creator of the universe and ruler of human history, an eternal Father

whom men can love and trust, a God of perfect righteousness who demands righteousness of man—for this
we must turn from Asia to the Near East and another
great stream of religious life entirely.

THE MIDDLE EASTERN STREAM

The earliest human civilization began in the Fer-
tile Crescent, which stretches in a great arc from the
Tigris and Euphrates valleys of Mesopotamia to the
Nile Valley of Egypt. Midway in that crescent, between
the Mediterranean Sea and the Arabian Desert, is a
tiny land the size of Vermont. It has been a bridge between the empires of Egypt and Mesopotamia, between the continents of Africa, Asia, and Europe, since
the beginning of human history. Caravans, armies,
refugees, and ideas moved up and down its roads.

This land is Palestine. In it began the three great religions of faith in one God, or monotheisms: Judaism,
Christianity, and Islam.

These three differ sharply among themselves. Yet
even Islam, which is set most clearly apart from the
other two, testifies to the bond between them. It calls
Christians and Jews "Peoples of the Book" rather than
"heathen" who have no scripture to reveal the nature
and the purpose of the one true God. The common
core of these related monotheistic faiths was worked
out by—or given to—the little community called Israel, which lived in or near Palestine during the two
thousand years before the Christian era began.

The story of Israel and its faith is found in what
Jews call the Bible; Christians, the Old Testament; and

Muslims, the Torah. In its main outlines the story is familiar to every religiously literate European and American. Its earliest episodes center around a Mesopotamian named Abraham who wandered west from the city of Ur about 1900 B.C. Later Abraham's descendants moved to the delta of the Nile during a famine period. Coming into disfavor as a foreign minority, they were enslaved and threatened with extinction. Then, in a desperate bid for freedom, they escaped. This exodus ever after seemed to Israel a miracle, testifying that their God had special concern for them and that he has power to turn the tide of history.

Three events connected with the exodus were decisive for Israel's faith: the crossing of the Red Sea in spite of Pharaoh's army; the encounter of Moses, the Israelite leader, with the God of Abraham who now revealed his name as Yahweh (Jehovah); and the receiving of a code of moral and religious laws—the Ten Commandments—by a great assembly at Mt. Sinai. From this point onward Israel believed itself to be bound with Yahweh in a special relationship called the Covenant. Yahweh, who they became convinced was the God of the whole universe, would lead, protect, and sustain them. In turn they were called upon to obey his will and commandments, loving him in their hearts and serving his purpose in the world. A generation after this covenant faith was established, Israel conquered a homeland, west of the Jordan River in Palestine. There, between 1200 and 1400 B.C., the Old Testament took shape, the first expression of the faith that underlies Judaism, Christianity, and Islam.

The Biblical Faith

The core of biblical faith is belief in a God of the universe who is personal. Israel discovered the Creator to be a "living God," with attributes like those that make up personality in man, though without the limitations of human existence.

. . . GOD IS PURPOSIVE

God intends something by what he does; he made the world for a reason. His creativity is not just the play of a dancing Siva. The prophet Jeremiah used the figure of a potter working at his wheel, creating a vessel of usefulness and beauty. "Like the clay in the potter's hand, so are you in my hand, O house of Israel."[2]

The story of Abraham's call to go out into a strange land, toward an unknown destiny, is full of this sense of the vast purpose of God. "Now the Lord said to Abram, 'Go from your country and your kindred and your father's house to the land that I will show you. And I will make of you a great nation, and I will bless you, and make your name great, so that you will be a blessing. I will bless those who bless you, and him who curses you I will curse; and by you all the families of the earth will bless themselves."[3]

. . . GOD IS JUST

God not only gives the moral law; he embodies it. Lofty, mystical language about the Ultimate may miss the point for, as Isaiah says:

. . . the Lord of hosts is exalted in justice,
and the Holy God shows himself holy in righteousness.[4]

WHEN FAITH MEETS FAITH

. . . GOD IS LOVING

Hosea the prophet heard God speak like a husband and like a father to his little child:

I will betroth you to me for ever; I will betroth you to me in righteousness and in justice, in steadfast love, and in mercy.

> When Israel was a child, I loved him,
> and out of Egypt I called my son.
>
> . . . .
>
> It was I who taught Ephraim to walk,
> I took them up in my arms; . . .
> I led them with cords of compassion,
> with the bands of love, . . .
> and I bent down to them and fed them.[5]

. . . MAN IS CENTRAL

Israel, finding God to be personal, like man, also found man to be stamped with the image of the divine. This divine image is not some hidden, secret self. It is revealed as man rightly exercises all his powers of body, mind, and spirit. Not for Israel the separation of soul and body, of inner life from outer. But neither is humanity merged with animal and physical nature. For at the creation God said:

"Let us make man in our image, after our likeness, and let them have dominion over the fish of the sea, the birds of the air, and over the cattle, and over all the earth."[6] And so, for biblical faith, the whole story of the world centers in mankind.

. . . HISTORY IS SIGNIFICANT

Because God is working through it, and because the men who make it reflect the image of God, human history is totally significant. Israel gave the world a sense of time by discovering that what happens in time is unique and final. It cannot be undone or done over. All the values that a life will ever achieve must be achieved here and now in the flow of everyday events. There is no *samsara* in biblical faith, no endless pattern of birth and rebirth, no pattern of history circling round and round, age after age. For Israel, history is a line that stretches from a beginning toward a goal. To find ourselves in motion along that line, partners with God, is to know salvation. For God is the source of all life, all vitality, prosperity, peace, and blessing.

> O Lord, how manifold are thy works!
> In wisdom hast thou made them all;
> the earth is full of thy creatures.
>
> . . . .
>
> These all look to thee,
> to give them their food in due season.
>
> . . . .
>
> . . . when thou takest away their breath, they
> die and return to their dust.
> When thou sendest forth thy Spirit, they are
> created;
> and thou renewest the face of the ground.[7]

. . . RIGHTEOUSNESS IS ESSENTIAL

Right relationship with God means blessing and life. But such a relationship has its price. That price is righteousness. To be sure, we are human and frail, and God knows how to forgive, yet the will to obey his commands must be present or no relationship with him is possible. And so morality lies at the heart of religion. Not sacrifice, not ritual, not mysticism nor philosophical understanding, but righteousness is the most important thing in the world. Cried Amos the shepherd prophet:

> . . . let justice roll down like waters,
> And righteousness like an ever-flowing stream.[8]

Biblical faith, then, is a matter of personal relationships: man related to his fellow man in love and justice; and man related to God through love and obedience. Micah condensed this essence of religion in a memorable verse:

> He has showed you, O man, what is good;
> and what does the Lord require of you
> but to do justice, and to love kindness,
> and to walk humbly with your God?[9]

The Biblical Faiths Today

Today the "Peoples of the Book," who have built their religions upon this common core of biblical faith, are far and away the most numerous and influential of all religious communities. Judaism numbers only a few million adherents, but it exercises an influence out of all proportion to its numbers. It is the most creative small minority in human history. Christianity, in all its branches, is twice as large as its nearest rival among the religions. It has some 800 million nominal adherents at least, one quarter or more of mankind. Islam is the second largest living faith with a constituency estimated to be about 435 million.

These monotheisms, moreover, are spread far more widely over the earth than other religions. Islam reaches in a great band from the pillars of Hercules in North Africa to Java in Indonesia. Christianity lives in churches that are now native to practically every country on all the continents.

The core of biblical faith has been developed in very different directions in these three religions. Members of one have sometimes called members of the others infidels and unbelievers. Now we direct our attention to each of these in turn to understand their distinctive messages.

Faith Meets Faith ✟ Harold looked around, vaguely aware that things were not quite as usual in chapel. Beside him Janie had stopped reading *Lady Chatterly's Lover,* and the fellow in front was no longer wiggling his ears. In fact the whole audience was uncommonly quiet and attentive. This guy, he thought, is really good.

"This guy" was Rabbi Gordis, one of the team of visitors during Religious Emphasis Week at Park Forest College. In the compulsory chapel service that day a panel of a minister, a priest, and a rabbi had the tough job of convincing their captive audience that religion is interesting and important in the modern world. The first two had tried hard, but chaos was quietly setting in. Then the rabbi came on. With a few deft comments and a quick joke, he began to lead his hearers by the hand down the road he wanted them to go.

In fact, Harold found himself entertaining an unexpected and somewhat shocking thought: "Suppose I weren't already a Baptist. Which one of these faiths would I join on the strength of today's performance? Why, I'd probably end up being a Jew!"

5 Judaism

ANY HONEST account of the realism and ethical vigor of Judaism is likely to make an excellent impression. That impression is reinforced by the miraculous history of the Jews. The "children of Israel" have been the toughest, most resilient, and most creative minority in human history.

Why is this? How does one account for these two facts: that the Jewish people, with the Jewish faith at the heart of their life, have been so successful both in surviving and in creating greatness; and that this faith has not spread widely but has remained the inheritance of a tiny minority? We may discover the answer if we look at three major points: Judaism's attitude toward mission, Judaism's history, and Judaism's embodiment in a particular "national" group.

JUDAISM'S ATTITUDE TOWARD OUTREACH

Judaism has never had much interest in winning converts. The rabbi who so impressed Harold in the college chapel neither expected nor wanted him to become a Jew and join his congregation. He wished only to persuade Christians and unbelievers to understand and respect his faith, to be friendly to his people, and to follow, in their own way, the high ideals of the Jewish way of life.

Even if a Gentile wished to enter Judaism, he would have to pass high barriers. Circumcision for males is the most familiar of these requirements. Jewish babies undergo this soon after birth, but for the adult convert this may be a painfully difficult procedure. The story of Genesis 34 is an ancient illustration of the problem.

And such a step is in no sense necessary for salvation. Rewards and punishments are given by God strictly in accord with the moral quality of one's life. A righteous non-Jew stands before God on exactly the same footing as a righteous Jew. Traditional Jewish literature has many passages concerning Gentiles who have won God's favor and a place in the world to come by acts of kindness and integrity.

JUDAISM'S HISTORY

Moreover, throughout most of a long history, Judaism has lived in such a hostile environment that attempts to convert others might be positively dangerous. They could bring down ghastly reprisals upon the entire Jewish community.

This subject of Jewish history is a painful one for Christians; at least, it ought to be. There has been so much organized persecution by churches and so much spontaneous mistreatment of Jews by church members, that Jews find it very difficult to take the claims of Christianity seriously. Here is the gist of that history:

A.D. 325—Christianity becomes the official religion of the Roman world. Judaism increasingly persecuted as the religion of those who rejected Christ.

The Middle Ages—Jews are shut up in ghettos, forced to wear peculiar dress, forbidden to follow normal occupations, subject to constant threat of violence from ignorant, envious, or fanatical Christian populations. Crusades lead to butchery of Jews. The Inquisition of the Roman Catholic Church is partly directed against them.

1290—Jews expelled by law from England.

1394—Expelled by law from France.

1492—Expelled by law from Spain.

Nineteenth century—Rise of modern anti-Semitism. Pogroms (massacres of Jews) in Russia, Poland, and elsewhere.

1933-1945—Period of Nazism with its attempt to exterminate the European Jew. About six million shot, burned, poisoned, gassed, clubbed, and starved to death.

No wonder the Jews remain a tiny minority! The wonder is that they remain at all. Yet we cannot stop at this point. After all, other great faiths have known persecution, too. Islam was born amid bitter hostility. Christianity began with a tiny handful of half-educated Palestinian peasants and faced violent opposition through much of its first three hundred years. Why did these great world religions grow though the faith from which they both came did not grow?

Here we confront a key point in understanding Judaism. One phrase has been appearing frequently, "the Jewish people." Judaism has been the religion of a national-racial group. Remember that the focus of Hebrew religion was Israel's experience of being drawn into a special relationship with God called the Covenant. One of the chief records of that experience is found in Deuteronomy 6. Here we find the only creed Judaism has ever had and the best summary of its faith. It is the famous *shema*, so called from the opening word in Hebrew:

Hear, O Israel: The Lord our God is one Lord; and you shall love the Lord your God with all your heart, and with all your soul, and with all your might.[1]

JUDAISM: A RELIGION OF RULES

What it means to love the Lord is indicated in the sentences that immediately follow the *shema*. "And these words which I command you this day shall be upon your heart; and you shall teach them diligently to your children, and shall talk to them when you sit in your house, and when you walk by the way, and when you lie down, and when you rise."[2]

By "these words" Deuteronomy refers to whole chapters of legal regulations concerning worship, diet, philanthropy, religious festivals, the priesthood, social justice, and social relations. Here are some examples of this legal instruction or Torah of God:

Only be sure that you do not eat the blood [of the animals you slaughter]; for the blood is the life, and you shall not eat the life with the flesh.[3]

Every animal that parts the hoof and has the hoof cloven in two, and chews the cud, among the animals, you may eat . . . the swine, because it parts the hoof but does not chew the cud, is unclean for you.[4]

You shall not boil a kid in its mother's milk.[5]

Observe the month of Abib, and keep the passover to the Lord your God; for in the month of Abib the Lord your God brought you out of Egypt by night.[6]

You shall appoint judges and officers in all your towns which the Lord your God gives you, according to your tribes; and they shall judge the people with righteous judgment.[7]

You shall not see your brother's ox or his sheep go astray, and withhold your help from them; you shall take them back to your brother.[8]

A woman shall not wear anything that pertains to a man, nor shall a man put on a woman's garment; for whoever does these things is an abomination to the Lord your God.[9]

To a foreigner you may lend upon interest, but to your brother you shall not lend upon interest.[10]

When a man is newly married, he shall not go out with the army or be charged with any business; he shall be free at home one year, to be happy with his wife whom he has taken.[11]

These are only a few of the rules contained in Deuteronomy. Exodus and Numbers have many more, and Leviticus has the most impressive collection of all. Altogether, here is an elaborate and impressive code that attempts to give a divine dimension and order to all aspects of life.

Nevertheless, life is so complicated and changing that no fixed code is ever able to cover all contingencies. The biblical laws needed constant interpretation

and reinterpretation. Just when is meat free enough
from blood to be lawful? Exactly what are the elements
of woman's clothing and man's clothing that may not
be interchanged? How is the Passover to be observed
properly? Scholars in the law or scribes, together with
rabbis or teachers who interpreted it to the common
people, worked endlessly to answer such questions.
Their opinions became a vast commentary on the
Torah by which it could be applied to every question
of daily life. Between 586 B.C. and A.D. 600, these materials were gathered into a vast compendium called
the Talmud (studies). Upon the Talmud traditional
Jewish life has been built. Its six major divisions and
sixty-three volumes cover every aspect of life with
authoritative teaching and advice. What it means to
be a member of the covenant people is defined here in
unmistakable fashion. It means having a prescribed
way in which to perform every act of every day. All
of life is to be "sanctified," made holy by being pat-
terned according to God's will.

On wakening and before stirring, the Orthodox Jew
prays a prescribed prayer. Each act in the process of
getting up has its own ordained blessing to recite: on
washing hands and face, on setting foot to the ground,
on attending to bodily needs, on donning underclothes
fringed as commanded by the Torah. He prepares for
worship by wrapping himself in a large fringed prayer
shawl. Next, a little box containing Scripture passages
is fastened to his left arm and another to his forehead.
Thus he fulfills the commandment of Deuteronomy:
"You shall bind them as a sign upon your hand, and

they shall be as frontlets between your eyes."[12] With each motion appropriate benedictions are recited. Morning worship occupies nearly an hour. Only then is it time for breakfast, after hands are washed and a benediction spoken. Grace follows each meal, with formal worship being held again in the afternoon and at dusk. Between times, benedictions are ordained for almost every kind of occurrence—a between meals snack, trying on a new garment, a taste of fruit, the sight of lightning, an encounter with a learned man, the coming of good news or bad. Just before sleep the day ends, as it began, with prayer.

Add to this picture the complex rules governing diet, by which only kosher foods are eaten—and in the right order and way. Foods containing milk must never be prepared in vessels used for foods containing meat; nor can these two kinds of food be eaten within a certain interval of time. Thus has tradition spelled out the meaning of the law, "You shall not boil a kid in its mother's milk." There are numerous rules for observance of the Sabbath, for dress, for all kinds of social relationships.

Obviously, Judaism as practiced in the full scope of its ritual is a highly specialized way of life. To conform to it one must almost learn it from childhood, as any culture is learned. Indeed, a practicing Jew will describe himself as a person of two cultures—the American culture, for example, in which he lives as a citizen; and the Jewish culture in which he lives as an individual, a family member, and a member of the Jewish community.[13]

JUDAISM TODAY

Today there are about 13 million Jews on earth. Almost every country has at least a few, but the United States has more than any other. The over five million American Jews make up the richest and possibly the most influential Jewish community, with New York as the largest Jewish city in the world (it is also the largest Negro city and the largest Irish city!). Other large Jewish communities are found in Israel, of course, and in Soviet Russia, where there are an estimated two and a half million Jews. In the latter, all Jewish organizations except synagogues are banned and Jews are subject to considerable harassment.

Judaism in Europe and America—and Israel—exhibits great diversity. A perennial topic of discussion in Jewish periodicals is the question, "What is a Jew?" In spite of a recent rise in religious affiliation, some estimates would indicate that nearly half of the American Jewish community is "nonreligious." Such persons are identified, both by themselves and by others, as belonging to the social and cultural group called Judaism but observe few if any of the ritual practices prescribed by Torah and Talmud.

American Jews who do practice their faith are divided into three major groups. The largest, perhaps two million strong, is called Orthodox. Here observance of the traditional Jewish way of life is at a maximum. Most of the elaborate worship is conducted in Hebrew. Regulations regarding kosher food, the rules governing the Sabbath, the separation of men and women in worship, and similar prescriptions are accepted just as fully as possible. Torah, as set forth in the traditional formulations, is believed to be the very word and will of God, unchanged and unchanging.

At the other extreme in point of view is Reform Judaism. Usually distinguishable by the fact that their places of worship are called temples rather than synagogues, Reform Jews pay relatively little attention to the traditional letter of the law. Correspondingly greater emphasis is laid upon the prophets of Israel. The twin tests of reason and conscience are applied to each belief and requirement of Judaism: does it make sense? does it have any moral significance? Scientific critical methods are applied to study of the Bible and of Jewish tradition and history. Services of worship are almost entirely in English. Kosher food regulations are largely ignored.

Between Orthodoxy and Reform stands a third group, called Conservative Judaism. Here traditional faith and practice are valued for the continuity they provide with the history of the Jewish people. Yet there is a recognition that many adjustments need to be made, both in the practice of Judaism and in religious thought. There is an attempt to hold on to the tradition as far as possible, and to make necessary modifications slowly and within the framework of the law if that can be done. Both Hebrew and English are used in worship.

Having glanced at the divisions in modern Judaism, let us now try to get a sense of the spirit common to them all. Four hallmarks of the Jewish approach to life are stamped upon all the adherents of this faith:

Its Respect for Learning

Judaism has lived "by the book" in a way that few religions have. Driven into the ghetto and deprived of most normal outlets for their creative energies, Jews found in scholarship the highest and most satisfying vocation. The rabbi, as a religious leader, has always been a scholar and a teacher rather than a priest.

After the French Revolution, European Jewry found its liberation from the ghetto. The whole world of modern knowledge suddenly lay open to young Jews whose tradition had created in them an intense love of learning. The result was an explosion of Jewish talent in literature, science, philosophy, and the arts. To this day the image of the rabbi as a superbly educated man, the extremely high educational expectations of the average Jewish family, and the intellectual creativity of Jews, all reflect a love and respect for learning.

Its Stress on Action

Even in Orthodox Judaism, observance of the Law is more basic than any particular set of beliefs about the God who gave it. Jeremiah wrote: "Thus saith the Lord of hosts, the God of Israel: 'Me they have forsaken and they have not kept my law!'" An ancient Talmudic commentary interprets that verse: "Would that men forsook Me," says God, "if only they kept my law."[14] Judaism has never had any formal creed as a

74

test of orthodoxy. In a notable symposium of modern Jewish intellectuals, only two out of thirty-one made a point of insisting that belief in God is essential to Judaism, and these two commented on the extreme difficulty of such belief![15]

This is not to say that Judaism has not had its share of God-intoxicated men, mystics, and devout believers. If theology is understood as "teaching about God," (*theos*—God; *logia*—teaching), then a Jew, Martin Buber, is one of the greatest theologians of the twentieth century. Nevertheless, it is true that where Christianity characteristically emphasizes faith, Judaism emphasizes action. Whereas worship in a church is primarily designed to call men's attention to an invisible world of spiritual reality, a synagogue service points, above all, to the way in which men should live in this world.

Its Ethical Sensitivity

The trumpet call of the Hebrew prophets for justice and mercy has never ceased to ring through Judaism. The Jewish need to aid one another in battling with a hostile environment has reinforced the philanthropic impulse. Consequently, Jews probably give more per capita to help others—both Jews and Gentiles—than any other religious community.

Mercy is not enough, however, in the mind of Judaism. Justice is essential. Indeed, righteousness in relations between man and man will eliminate much of the need for charity. From the Jewish community has come an unending series of fighters for social morality—

critics, reformers, and revolutionaries. In most American communities Jewish leadership is prominent in civic causes and liberal crusades.

Its This-worldly Character

"Hear, O Israel, the Lord our God is one." This unity of God is taken to symbolize a unity running throughout all things. Basic in many religions is a list of contrasts, like this:

> body and soul
> daily life and religious life
> matter and spirit
> time and eternity
> faith and reason
> this world and the world to come
> earth and heaven.

Judaism recognizes these as different but not as opposites, not even as separated. They belong together, within the unity of the one God who created them all. True religion is not separation from daily life but the sanctification, the "making holy," of daily life. The world and the flesh are not temptations but blessings to be enjoyed to the full in the way God intended. He made them for the pleasure and well-being of man, and it is not only foolish but actually a sin to spurn his good gifts. The aim of religion is not to prepare man for another way of life beyond the grave or in another world. It is to make his life in this world righteous, happy, fruitful, and faithful. The other world will take care of itself if this world and its possibilities are rightly used.

Some words from the greatest Jewish thinker of our day illuminate this understanding of the world:

> To look away from the world, or to stare at it, does not help a man to reach God; but he who sees the world in Him stands in His presence.
>
> I know nothing of a "world" and a "life in the world" that might separate a man from God. . . . He who truly goes out to meet the world goes out also to God.[16]

Faith Meets Faith ✝ Nancy blinked and looked again at her textbook. Sure enough, the list began:

Name	Place of Origin	Founder	Year
Catholic Church	Jerusalem	Jesus Christ	33

Below it were ranged other churches—Baptist, Methodist, Presbyterian, and the rest—each with its founder and his date. Her own Lutheran Church was listed as having been founded in Germany by Martin Luther in 1517. That was many centuries away from the beginnings of Christianity. No connection with Jesus Christ was indicated. A little shaken, she turned a page and began to read more about the complex beliefs and the tremendous claims of the church that calls itself Catholic, or sometimes Roman Catholic.

An advertisement had caught Nancy's eye and invited her into this encounter. "What Do Catholics Believe About the Bible?" it asked in bold type. Persuasively the ad outlined the Roman Catholic position and suggested that for those who wished to know more about authentic Christianity a free correspondence course was available. Nancy was intrigued. Now, just one week after sending in her name, she had the first lesson in hand. And already the question had crossed her mind, "Could it be that this is the original and authentic Christian Church?"

6 Christianity

MILLIONS of Catholics are not Roman. Yet with all the differences and rivalries among the various Catholic churches, they bear a distinct family resemblance. Together they represent an ancient and impressive form of the Christian faith. To what we may call the Catholic emphasis in Christianity we shall direct our major, though not exclusive, attention in this chapter.

To understand and judge the claims of Catholic Christianity, we must ask how it arose. The Christian movement, of which the Catholic churches are a part, traces its ancestry to the Old Testament. In this it is like Judaism, at which we looked in the previous chapter, and like Islam to which we shall turn next. Christians are one of the "Peoples of the Book." To understand their faith, however, something more than the Old Testament is necessary, for Christianity rests upon a New Testament as well as an Old. To these original documents of the Christian faith we must now turn.

CHRISTIANITY IS BORN

The first and greatest of the history books that recount the origins of the Christian church has two volumes. The first is called "The Gospel According to Luke"; the second, "The Acts of the Apostles." The story they tell is probably known, in outline at least, to more people than any other in all human history. Here is the gist of it:

A Jewish baby named Joshua (in Greek this name becomes Jesus) was born into a humble home in Palestine. When he was about thirty years old, he became involved in a religious revival sparked by a man called John the Baptizer. Jesus himself was baptized. Almost immediately he too began to preach. His message was simple but dramatic: "The time is fulfilled, and the kingdom of God is at hand; repent, and believe in the gospel."[1]

Those were days of intense expectation of the Messiah, the Anointed One. People believed that God was about to act in a new way. Their hopes were confirmed as they saw Jesus demonstrating an amazing power to heal the sick in mind and body. From his lips they heard teaching of originality and power. Sometimes it came in short pithy sayings that carried a world of meaning: "Love your enemies. Do good to those who hate you. Bless those who curse you. Pray for those who abuse you. To him who strikes you on the cheek, offer the other also. And from him who takes away your cloak do not withhold your coat as well. . . . As you wish that men would do to you, do so to them."[2]

80

Often Jesus taught by unforgettable stories: "A man was going down from Jerusalem to Jericho, and he fell among robbers, who stripped him and beat him, and departed, leaving him half-dead. . . . " And so on, until the image of the good Samaritan was stamped forever on the mind of humanity.[3]

So winning, in fact, were the words of Jesus, so compelling the power of his life, that some began to see in him the expected Messiah! At the same time, however, opposition was hardening. Jewish leaders bitterly resented the liberties he took with the Torah. He made influential enemies by condemning the commercialized temple worship in Jerusalem. By associating with disreputable people, he scandalized the puritanical. Opposition came to a head at Passover time about A.D. 30. Jesus was charged with blasphemy and fomenting rebellion. Roman soldiers executed him. Practically all his friends deserted him at the end.

But within three days some of those wavering followers had become convinced that Jesus was not dead after all. On more than one occasion, they saw him and talked with him. After a few weeks the appearances ceased. Then, just fifty days after they had first seen the risen Jesus, there came a tremendous burst of faith among his friends and a burning compulsion to share that faith with all the world. Uncertainty was replaced by absolute conviction that Jesus was indeed the Messiah and that in him God had actually started to bring in a New Age. The heart of the disciples' message was proclaimed by Peter on the day called Pentecost.

"Repent," said Peter, "and be baptized every one of you in the name of Jesus Christ for the forgiveness of your sins; and you shall receive the gift of the Holy Spirit. For the promise is to you and to your children, and to all that are far off, every one whom the Lord our God calls to him."[4]

Three major points in this message mark the road by which Christianity moved out of Judaism and became an independent faith, destined to develop into the most widespread and influential spiritual movement of all history.

"Be baptized in the name of Jesus Christ." Jesus is the Messiah. (*Christ* is simply the Greek translation of *Messiah* and means the same thing, "anointed.") This man had been an utter failure in ordinary human terms, rejected by his own people and crucified as a criminal. Nevertheless, he was the person chosen by God to make his rule effective on earth in a new way, and to bring men into a new relationship with himself. In support of this interpretation, Jesus' disciples pointed to certain passages in the prophetic writings of the Old Testament itself:

> Surely he has borne our griefs
>   and carried our sorrows; . . .
> he was wounded for our transgressions,
>   he was bruised for our inquities;
> upon him was the chastisement that made us whole,
>   and with his stripes we are healed.[5]

"For the forgiveness of your sins." Like all good Jews the early Christians took questions of right and wrong very seriously. God's judgment upon those who

transgressed his Law haunted their minds, but they became convinced that in Jesus God had shown a new way to deal with sin. Men are not saved by strenuous attempts to keep a Law. The starting point must be trust in that forgiving love of God which Jesus revealed in his life and death. "Therefore, since we are justified by faith, we have peace with God through our Lord Jesus Christ."[6]

"The promise is to you and to your children and to all that are far off, every one whom the Lord our God calls to him." Here is another conviction that marked off the early Christians from the Jews who shared the same Bible with them (there was no New Testament for at least one hundred years after Jesus' death): God's intention is to call not just one people but all peoples into covenant with himself.

It was in their experiences with the risen Jesus that his disciples were given a fundamental directive on this crucial point. All the stories of the resurrection agree: the risen Jesus' message to his followers was a command to undertake a world-wide mission. Matthew's account is probably the best known:

And Jesus came and said to them, "All authority in heaven and on earth has been given to me. Go therefore and make disciples of all nations, baptizing them in the name of the Father and of the Son and of the Holy Spirit, teaching them to observe all that I have commanded you; and lo, I am with you always, to the close of the age."[7]

The first significant attempt to implement this commission seems to have occurred in the Syrian city of

Antioch. Here Christian refugees preached directly to "Greeks" and received a warm response. This story in Acts 11 ends with the phrase: "And in Antioch the disciples were for the first time called Christians." In one moment the new faith had found both its mission and its name!

CATHOLIC CHRISTIANITY DEVELOPS

Powered by a missionary spirit, Christianity spread rapidly. At first it was popular chiefly among slaves and other lower classes. After severe early persecution followed by even more savage attacks in the third century, the Emperor Constantine gave it secure legal status in A.D. 313. It traveled east as well as west—perhaps as far as India—and south into Africa. By the year 400 it had become the official religion of the empire and had developed the dominant characteristics of what is still called Catholic Christianity.

"Catholic" originally meant simply "universal," a fact that Protestants remember as they repeat the phrase in the Apostles' Creed, "I believe in the holy catholic church." By a natural evolution, this also came to mean "orthodox," the standard form of Christianity against which to measure all heresies and deviations. By A.D. 500 this widely practiced standard form of Christianity could be recognized by three chief marks: an authoritative organization or church order, worship centered in the sacraments, and a sharply defined theology. To this day these distinguish the many branches of Catholicism: Anglican, Russian or Greek Orthodox, Roman, South Indian, Egyptian, Armenian, and others.

CATHOLIC CHURCH ORDER

From the many forms of ministry mentioned in the New Testament, there evolved a definite threefold scheme of deacons, elders or priests, and bishops. The bishop was superintendent of all the Christians in one city and in the rural area attached to it. His authority in church administration was great, for he was considered a direct successor of the apostles to whom Jesus had entrusted the administration of the church (as Matthew 16:19 was interpreted). Even more fundamental was his role as teacher and guardian of sound faith. All the bishops gathered in council were considered the final and infallible authority on matters of Christian belief. These councils of bishops shaped such fundamental summaries of Christian doctrine as the Nicene Creed.

Central, then, to any Catholic system is the bishop, who stands in a line of succession believed to go directly back to the twelve apostles. He alone ordains men to the priesthood. Upon him depends the whole system of sacramental life that is administered by the clergy.

CATHOLIC SACRAMENTS

For Catholicism, the great reality is not so much individual experience as the corporate life of the Christian community. A member of the church is a member of the mystical body of Christ. Christ's life continues unbroken through centuries and includes those in heaven as well as those now living on earth. This

85

church, in itself, is divine and infallible, no matter what errors may afflict its members. It is primarily in the church that the love and grace of God are active. Within the church certain channels are designated for the flow of grace. Called sacraments, these are seven in number. Available only through the ministry of a priest who is related properly to his bishop, the holy sacraments are the Catholic's spiritual meat and drink.

Baptism

By consecrated water applied in the name of the Trinity, the terrible curse of original sin is taken away and the Catholic launched on his life in the church.

Confirmation

Following initiation into the body of Christ by baptism, the Catholic is strengthened by a sacrament that is believed to impart the Holy Spirit and bring strength for living as a Christian.

Eucharist

Chief of the sacraments and center of Catholic worship is the rite based on the Last Supper Jesus had with his disciples. His words over the bread and wine, "This is my body which is for you" and "This cup is the new covenant in my blood"[8] are taken quite literally. Jesus is held to be really present in the consecrated elements, on the altar and in the bodies of those who receive communion.

Penance

Texts like John 20:23 are cited as indicating the priest's power of forgiveness: "If you forgive the sins of any, they are forgiven; if you retain the sins of any, they are retained." To the word of absolution is attached "penance," a requirement that helps atone for the wrongdoing and takes the place of God's punishment.

Extreme Unction

To sustain the Catholic in grave illness and in the hour of death, a sacrament is given by anointing with consecrated oil. It is based on James 5:14, which speaks of praying for the sick and anointing with oil, presumably to cure them. However, the Catholic sacrament now is primarily intended to prepare the soul for eternity.

Marriage

In this sacrament a man and woman bind themselves together until death, with a priest as witness, and are given grace to discharge the responsibilities of family life.

Holy Orders

This is the sacrament by which a man is made a priest, and given authority to administer the other sacraments and to take leadership in the life of the church. Ordination, by a bishop in the "apostolic succession," marks a man for life.

87

CATHOLIC BELIEF

During the first four hundred years of Christian history there was a tremendous ferment of theological ideas. All kinds of interpretations competed for acceptance. Assaulted by such a variety of opinions, the church defended itself by trying to define a standard or orthodox position on all fundamental questions of faith.

As successors to the apostles, the bishops took the lead in defining these necessary beliefs or dogmas. The ecumenical creeds are the result of such councils of bishops and have provided the basis for most orthodox Christianity down to the present day. The most important of these are the Nicene and the Chalcedonian creeds. These defined the two beliefs by which Christians have most generally been distinguished from other "Peoples of the Book"—the belief that God is three persons, not one; and the belief that Jesus Christ is both God and man.

The Nicene Creed was framed in A.D. 325 to refute the Arian heresy, which holds that there is one supreme being, God, and that Christ is a subordinate divinity, much higher than man but not fully God. No, said the bishops, Christ is "God of God, light of light, very God of very God; begotten not made, being of one substance with the Father. . . ." And to this affirmation was added a confession of faith in the Holy Spirit, "The Lord and Giver of Life, who proceedeth from the Father and the Son; who with the Father and Son together is worshipped and glorified. . . ." Thus the doctrine of the Trinity was nailed to the mast of the church.

But if Jesus Christ is truly God, how is he related to mankind? Was the human Jesus of the gospels, who walked, taught, ate, drank, and died in Palestine, only an illusion? To that question the creed formulated in A.D. 451 by the Council of Chalcedon gave this reply:

[We] acknowledge one and the same Son, our Lord Jesus Christ, at once complete in Godhead and complete in manhood; truly God and truly man . . . ; as regards his Godhead, begotten of the Father before the ages, but yet as regards his manhood begotten for us men and for our salvation, of Mary the Virgin, the God-bearer; according to the manhood; one and the same Christ, Son, Lord Only-begotten, recognized in two natures, without confusion, without change, without division, without separation; the distinction of natures being in no way annulled by the union, but rather the characteristics of each nature being preserved and coming together to form one person and subsistence, not as parted or separated into two persons, but one and the same Son and Only-begotten God the Word. . . .

Complicated? Perhaps, but it shows how Catholic Christianity took the road of careful, almost hair-splitting precision in order to safeguard the faith. These quotations from the creeds also reveal something else about Catholic theology: its marriage of biblical thought with Greek philosophy. Terms like "one substance" and "subsistence" are unintelligible in English. They have to be translated back into Greek—*homoousion* and *hypostasis*—and read in the light of Plato, Aristotle, and their successors. One might raise this question about Catholic theology: what happens when the Greek way of understanding the world is replaced by something else—by a philosophy based on modern science, for example?

Perhaps the Catholic answer lies in the word *tradition*. Authority lies not in the Bible as one may read and understand it, but in the mind of the whole Christian community. This experience of the community, its way of thinking and acting, is its tradition. Such tradition is not a dead, fixed authority but lives and changes with the experience of the community. This reliance on living tradition explains a great mystery: how Catholic churches can appear so utterly removed from the simplicity of the New Testament church, yet claim to be the original and authentic form of Christianity.

VARIETIES OF CHRISTIANITY

Up to now we have spoken as if Catholicism were one. In reality, many different churches claim such catholic elements as a hierarchy of bishops and priests, an emphasis on sacramental life, and a theology anchored in the Nicene and Chalcedonian Creeds. Two giant branches of Catholicism are dominant: Orthodoxy and Roman Catholicism.

Orthodoxy

When the Roman Empire began to split some four hundred years after Christ, the church split also. It developed two centers, one at Rome and the other at the eastern capital, Constantinople. The final break came about 1054. From then on, Eastern Christianity developed as a series of national churches called Orthodox: Russian, Serbian, Bulgarian, Greek, and Rumanian. All looked up to the Patriarch of Constantinople, yet all were quite independent. The Russian church grew larger than all the others put together, and the Moscow Patriarch became something of a rival to the Greek Patriarch. Today these churches, with their daughter churches made up largely of Eastern European immigrants in countries such as the United States, and such independent ancient churches as the Armenian and Syrian Orthodox, represent a family of perhaps 100 million Christians (the number depending largely on how one estimates the strength of Orthodoxy in Russia. A common estimate is 50 million.)

Four characteristics of Orthodoxy are most important.

. . . ITS WILLINGNESS TO CO-OPERATE

Most Orthodox churches are members of the World Council of Churches, the Russian Church having joined in 1961. In America several Orthodox churches are active in the work of the National Council of the Churches of Christ in the U.S.A. Orthodox bodies do not insist on agreement in doctrine before they work with other Christian groups.

. . . ITS SPLENDOR OF WORSHIP

Central to Orthodox life is a wonderfully elaborate and beautiful liturgical tradition, replete with music, symbolism, art, and pageantry. Orthodoxy is probably understood better by feeling than by thinking. It is the participation of one's whole being in adoration of the infinitely glorious God rather than acceptance of precise doctrinal formulations.

. . . ITS CONSERVATISM

Orthodox Christians believe their faith and worship preserve unchanged the tradition of the earliest centuries. They repudiate all changes in doctrine that have occurred since the first eight ecumenical councils, as well as the Roman Catholic view that Christian teaching may develop and add new dogmas. Unchanged and unchanging are favorite words likely to be heard in any conversation with the Orthodox.

. . . ITS EMPHASIS ON THE CHRISTIAN COMMUNITY

In spite of its Catholic-patterned priesthood, Orthodoxy stresses the unity of lay members and clergy in the wholeness of the church. The church is the living body of Christ, in which all have their proper part. In fact, most Orthodox theologians are laymen, not priests.

Roman Catholicism

Since nearly half the Christians in the world belong to a church that has its center in Rome, it is no wonder that the term "Catholic" is often used for a denomination that more properly ought to be called "Roman Catholic." Thirty million American "R.C.'s," and perhaps ten times that number throughout the earth, constitute the most powerful, active, and widespread body of Christians. This church springs from the Western branch of ancient Catholicism but has developed its own unique personality. It was partly in the struggle with Protestants in the sixteenth century that the modern Church of Rome developed such features as these:

. . . EMPHASIS ON AUTHORITY AND LAW

Much of the ancient Roman genius for organization is visible in the Roman Catholic Church. From its great world center in the Vatican, an intricate network spreads through lines of communication, of consultation, of control. From the Pope as head, through the cardinals, archbishops, and clergy of many lower ranks, the "chain of command" is definite and firm. Doctrine is organized in the same way; it is clear, precise, specific. Willingness to accept the authority of his church is the essential characteristic of a Roman Catholic.

. . . INFALLIBILITY OF THE POPE

From ancient times the Bishop of Rome claimed to be in a special sense successor to Peter, leader of the apostles, and hence leader of all bishops and thus of the whole church. In 1870 a Vatican Council declared that the Bishop of Rome (called Pope from the Latin *pappa*, "father") possesses not only governing authority over the church but the power to define dogma or essential belief without the possibility of error. In 1950 papal infallibility was invoked to define a new dogma, the Assumption of the Virgin Mary.

. . . VENERATION OF MARY

All Catholic churches have cultivated great devotion to Mary, the mother of Jesus, as the prevalence of the Madonna in Catholic art makes clear. But in the Roman Church, popular devotion has centered on Mary to an extraordinary degree, in the use of the rosary with its repeated "Hail Marys," in emphasis upon the "Sacred Heart of Mary," and in many other ways. In theology there has been a corresponding tendency to give Mary a central place in the plan of salvation, making her virtually a coredeemer with Christ. The dogma of the Assumption of the Virgin requires Roman Catholics to believe that Mary was taken up bodily at her death, to reign as queen in heaven.

. . . THEOLOGY AND PHILOSOPHY OF THOMAS AQUINAS

This greatest scholar of the Middle Ages worked out an amazing system of thought combining Christian belief with the philosophy of Aristotle. Thomism is now the official intellectual framework of Roman Catholic theology and philosophy. Working at all intellectual problems with the ideas of Aristotle-interpreted-by-Aquinas gives a special quality to Roman Catholic thought. One example is its interpretation of the Eucharist as "transubstantiation."

. . . TRANSUBSTANTIATION

Not content to affirm that Christ is really present in the bread and wine of the altar, Roman Catholic theology explains exactly how this is so. Any thing, it says, is composed of two parts: the "accidents," which are perceivable characteristics such as taste, color, shape, and smell; and the "substance," which is the inner essence—the "breadness" of the bread, the "wineness" of the wine. Usually substance and accidents go together. Bread usually tastes and looks like bread. Nevertheless, in the Mass, when the priest says, *"Hoc est corpus meum*" (This is my body), the substance of bread is replaced by the substance of Christ's flesh. An inner transubstantiation occurs though the outward characteristics of bread remain the same. Actually, in Roman theology the substance of Christ's blood is also created under the accidents of the bread. Even though the priest alone is allowed to drink of the Eucharist wine, those who receive the communion bread thus receive both the flesh and blood of Christ.

. . . USE OF LATIN

The Church of Rome uses Latin, the language of ancient Rome, for its chief services and official documents and as a medium of communication among all its branches. For a large organization this has obvious practical value, though there are some disadvantages in securing full lay participation in worship.

. . . MONASTIC ORDERS

In addition to more than a quarter of a million ordained clergy at work in parishes and dioceses, it has about 120,000 ordained "religious," (members of monastic orders) plus lay members of such orders totalling well over a million. These Jesuits, Franciscans, Sisters of St. Joseph, Ursuline Nuns, and members of over a thousand other communities serve as a flexible task force for all kinds of missionary work and church programs.

. . . EMPHASIS ON CELIBACY

Although other Catholic churches honor those who renounce marriage for the sake of religious service, the

Roman Church gives special honor to this act. All ordained clergy, for example, must be celibate. Married life is, theologically, a kind of second best. Indeed, all life in the world is less meritorious than the life of the clergy or the lay religious.

. . . RELIGIOUS BOOKKEEPING

Roman Catholic teaching places great stress on the idea of merit. The great problem is how to avoid punishment in hell or purgatory and to gain the joy of heaven. Jesus' death on the cross was to pay for our sins, and each time the Mass is celebrated that sacrifice takes place again and more credits are added to the church's treasury of grace. All the good works and sacrifices of the saints, too, go into that treasury. The Pope and the hierarchy have power to apply this accumulated merit to individuals who need it. This is called giving an indulgence, and it reduces the amount of penance or good works one must do to pay for his sins. It may also be secured for someone else, already in purgatory, to shorten his punishment. It was in outrage over the actions of certain priests in offering indulgences for money that Luther made the protest that touched off the Protestant Reformation. In addition to having the opportunity of drawing upon the treasury of grace that others have provided, the good Roman Catholic is urged to set up his own "bank account in heaven."[10] He can purchase happiness for his own future existence by accumulating supernatural merit during this life through observing the laws of the church, receiving the sacraments, and doing good works.

. . . POLITICAL AGGRESSIVENESS

Having been an official majority church for many centuries, the Roman Catholic communion tends to seek all the benefits that governments may grant, such as aid from the public treasury for its schools or grants from international aid programs for its missions. Rejecting the principle of the separation of church and state, it is not embarrassed to use political pressures to further its own interests.

One of its convictions is that efforts by a married couple to plan the size of their family by using mechanical or chemical methods of birth control are immoral. Therefore, the Roman Church works for laws to prevent use of such means, seeks to prevent their medical use in public hospitals, and obstructs government participation in programs dealing with the world population explosion.

A young person planning to marry a Roman Catholic should remember that if his partner wishes to remain a good member of that church, they must be married by a priest. That is possible only if there is a signed agreement that their children are to be raised as Roman Catholics. (If the Roman Catholic is an obedient church member, quite a few children may be born, since most methods of family planning are forbidden.)

Many Protestants ask, "What about missions to Roman Catholic countries?" There are many things to consider here. In such Roman Catholic areas as Latin America and the Philippines, church authorities themselves estimate that only about 10 per cent of the people are active communicants. For another thing, a monopoly position is easily abused, especially by a church with such an authoritative tradition as the Roman. Moreover, Roman Catholics of the United States send a higher proportion of their foreign missionaries to Latin America than do Protestants, making clear that it is indeed a mission field. It is also worth remembering that Roman Catholicism in some of these countries has lagged far behind in social attitudes, in morals, and in thought, compared with Roman Catholic communities in Britain, Germany, the United States, or Canada.

Protestant Christianity

Most of this book's readers will belong to that branch of the Christian community commonly called "Protestant." That name points to an extraordinary variety of groups, some of which refuse to accept it. (For instance, even though the official name of their church is "Protestant Episcopal," some Episcopalians feel themselves more a part of the Catholic family than the Protestant.) In the United States alone, more than 250 Protestant groups are noted by the religious census. Independent sects, subsects, and splinter congregations must number in the thousands.

Protestant is often given a negative meaning by being used as a blanket term to cover whatever is not Roman Catholic. The name did, in fact, arise from a protest offered by certain Lutheran princes during the sixteenth century German rebellion against the Church of Rome. But the term has a positive interpretation, often overlooked. From the Latin *pro* and *testare* ("for" and "witness"), it may be seen to refer to the act of standing for certain convictions.

Another name, "Reformed," often applied to many churches of this group, also indicates a determination not to submit to ancient abuses nor accept traditional heresies. Reformed churches believe in reshaping or reforming their church life and doctrine according to standards other than past usage.

A third name for this large group of Christians, numbering perhaps 150 million around the world and representing a distinct majority in the North American Christian community, is "Evangelical." Derived from the Greek word for gospel, *euangelion,* this name points to an insistence that all aspects of Christian belief or practice be based upon the gospel as set forth in the Scriptures, or at least subject to check and correction by the Bible. In North America, Evangelical is often used to mean the more conservative or more evangelistic Protestant groups but, in such places as Latin America, it is the preferred term for all Protestants.

The many varieties of Protestant faith and church life make it difficult to describe Protestantism in an adequate and acceptable way. Perhaps this is one reason why today the non-Roman sections of Christendom are deeply interested in finding greater unity through the ecumenical movement. The word *ecumenical,* from the Greek for "world-wide," today denotes world-wide Christianity. Through such a movement, which expresses itself in part through the World Council of Churches and national and local councils in many places, separate groups of Christians assert that they belong together. One by-product of this growing sense of unity has been an increasing interest in the organic union of denominations. In India as well as Canada, in the United States as well as Japan, this thrust toward greater visible unity is evident. Protestant Christians have taken a leading role in this development.

One way to get at the basic character of Protestant or evangelical Christianity is to consider the central event from which many, although not all, Protestants trace their spiritual ancestry—the Reformation of sixteenth century Europe. Great leaders like Martin Luther and John Calvin led much of Germany, France, Switzerland, Holland, Scandinavia, and Britain out of the existing church. Later these European Protestant communities also were planted in North America and around the world by the great missionary movement of the nineteenth century.

The Reformers protested against many of the very emphases that we have just listed as characteristic of Roman Catholicism; while, in reaction to their protest, the Roman Church redoubled those very emphases! Until recently Roman and Reformed Christianity have been growing farther apart. Fortunately, in our day the tide of division seems to be turning. A remarkable change set in when John XXIII became Pope in 1958. Unprecedented Roman interest in seeking understanding with the "separated brethren" was shown by the presence of official Vatican observers at the Assembly of the World Council of Churches at New Delhi in 1961. Official Protestant observers were invited to the Vatican Council that opened in 1962. Excellent

22929

books on the ecumenical movement by Roman Catholic scholars, visits to the Pope by leaders of the Church of England and the Church of Scotland, common observance of an annual Week of Prayer for Christian Unity, and other signs of spring give hope of a thaw in relationships that have been frozen almost solid since the sixteenth century.

Nevertheless, there remain sharp contrasts between Roman Catholic and Protestant positions. Some of the most important may be seen by comparing the following emphases with those given earlier for the Roman Church.

. . . CHRISTIAN FREEDOM AND LAY RESPONSIBILITY

Most Protestant churches are democratically governed by elected representatives. Often individual congregations are quite free of control by their denomination, and co-operation is voluntary. Protestant congregations have, in fact, been important training schools for modern political democracy. Moreover, the Christian life is conceived as a free response to the love of God, not as conforming to an elaborate set of religious rules. One of Luther's greatest books was his *Christian Liberty*. Here he pointed out that the Christian is freed by his faith from all earthly authority and law; but that he is bound, at the same time, in loving service to his fellow men, by his voluntary and joyful acceptance of God's saving love.

. . . THE FALLIBILITY OF ALL THINGS HUMAN

All authority must be tested, since no man or church is infallible. Luther's two tests for truth, when he was

101

ordered by the Emperor to retract and submit to the Roman Church, were "Scripture and right reason." Put another way, Protestants believe that only God is utterly reliable. All human authority is likely to be corrupted by our sinfulness and the natural limitations of our understanding. Protestants have applied this principle not only to church organizations and traditions, but also to governments, political parties, and social ideologies that set themselves up as worthy of a confidence that is dangerously close to absolute trust and obedience.

. . . CHRIST ALONE AS SAVIOR

Catholicism suggests that we need mediators or middlemen to help us in our relations with God. The saints, especially Mary, are expected to intercede for us and secure God's forgiveness and favor. Protestants insist that what the gospel is all about is God's own intervention, direct and immediate, in human history through Christ, so that no other mediator or intercessor is needed. While the great heroes and heroines of faith are honored, they are not given the kind of attention which suggests that what God has done in Christ is inadequate.

. . . THE NEED FOR CONSTANT THOUGHT

Unending re-examination of the meaning of our faith in the light of Scripture and of modern knowledge is characteristic of Protestantism, rather than any official philosophy based on ancient authorities. To be sure, Protestantism has its traditional authorities. Confessional churches, such as the Lutheran and some Reformed bodies, place special stress on historic statements of faith or "confessions." Others, such as Baptists and Congregationalists, reject the authority of any written creed. But all agree that no traditional system of thought is permanently binding in the way that Roman Christianity has made Aristotle-through-Aquinas, and Orthodoxy, the fourth through the tenth centuries. Most Protestants feel that the new knowledge and insight of every age must be used creatively to illuminate the essential and unchanging message of the Bible.

. . . PREACHING OF THE GOSPEL BY
     WORD AND SACRAMENT

Proclamation is central for Protestant worship, as over against the Catholic emphasis on ritual. In one sense the great sacrament for Protestants is the sermon, for here, in the physical activity of speaking, there is retold the spiritual story of God's love revealed in Christ, so that the listener's heart is warmed to loving and trusting response and his mind instructed about practical ways to put his faith into action.

The only divine grace that the Protestant recognizes is the personal love which God extends to him and to which he must respond in a personal and willing way. To him the idea of a grace communicated mechanically or automatically through sacraments is magical and superstitious. Protestants generally recognize two sacraments or ordinances as having New Testament authorization: baptism and the Lord's Supper. But these are taken as visible signs of God's grace, rather than as channels through which the divine presence or favor is dispensed. Like preaching, the sacraments are ways of making God's righteousness known, believed, and trusted.

This does not mean that Protestants take the sacraments lightly. True, they are relatively unimportant to some and entirely omitted by others, including Quakers and the Salvation Army. But their importance is understood in a different way than in Roman Catholicism. No Protestants hold that in the Lord's Supper the substance of Christ's body and blood replaces the substance of bread and wine. Yet many believe just as firmly as do Catholics in the "real presence" of Christ. It is, however, a presence that depends on the free grace of God rather than on a sacramental miracle.

. . . THE NEED FOR UNDERSTANDING

Protestants from the beginning have emphasized the use of understandable language and forms in worship. This fits the Protestant insistence that whenever anything of importance happens in religion it happens through genuine personal response to God. Therefore, the whole congregation should sing the hymns, and the sermon and the prayers should be understood by all.

This stress upon the use of plain language led to such characteristic Protestant activities as Bible translation. Luther's Bible, for instance, actually helped create the modern German language. Christian education and the Sunday school movement are other illustrations of the Protestant concern for understanding in religion.

. . . THE PRIESTHOOD OF ALL BELIEVERS

This emphasis, coupled with stress on Christian responsibility in daily life, replaces the Catholic tendency to separate religion from secular life through priestly celibacy and monastic orders. In fact, ordination to the ministry is not a sacrament for Protestants, but only a practical means of setting apart specially trained and capable individuals for particular functions in the church. But every Christian is a priest, able to have direct personal access to God through prayer, study, and faith. Moreover, he must be a priest to his neighbor, helping him to know God.

Life in church occupations is no more "religious" or holy than life in business, the home, or school. What God wants is obedience, love, and faith; and these are needed even more in the midst of worldly life than inside the church, if one must choose. One of the first acts of the Reformers was to marry, in order to indicate that celibacy has no special religious value. They taught that every home should be a little congregation of faith. A father, mother, or nursemaid serves God more truly in faithful and loving care of others than do those who may enter an artificial community of so-called religious devotion in order to escape such tasks.

. . . BY FAITH ALONE

Protestantism is rooted in the conviction that we are saved by faith in God's righteous love, not by those good works of our own that receive so much stress in the Roman Catholic system. This does not mean that

Protestants do not care about morality or hard work. Quite the opposite. Critics often charge us with being too moralistic, too much devoted to strenuous effort. But for Protestants, ethical effort and hard work carry no religious value in the sense of persuading God to accept us and reward us. With all that we can do, we still fall far short of meriting God's love. Our selfishness and perversity go too deep to be overcome by effort on our part. Moreover, God needs no cajoling. Our salvation was his idea before it was ours. He took the initiative in establishing the Covenant of old; he took the initiative in all that Christ did. His love is not for sale. It is freely offered to those who believe in him, take his will as their own, and entrust themselves to his purposes.

Luther's battle cry was *sola fide*. "By faith alone" are we justified—that is, forgiven and considered "just" or acceptable by God. His righteousness is not primarily judgment or condemnation. It is an infinite goodness that wills the salvation of all men and only waits for them to receive it in faith, love, and obedience. With such a basic conviction, Protestantism has no use for religious bookkeeping and the ideas of penance (as distinct from repentance), merit, indulgence, and reliance upon the saints.

As we have seen, there are all kinds of Protestants. Many of them, such as the numerous Baptists, Methodists of one persuasion or another, and the varied Pentecostal groups, do not trace their faith so directly to the Lutheran or Calvinistic Reformation as to other movements, some reaching far back into the Middle Ages and some of more recent times. But practically all would find themselves described by the emphases we have considered: Christians who center their faith in free obedience and loving trust toward the God and Father of Jesus Christ, and in responsive love toward their neighbor.

Faith Meets Faith ✝ Gerry and Ed stepped out into the blinding June sunshine. The great Riverside Church organ still sounded in their ears.

"This is really the cathedral of American Protestantism, isn't it," Gerry said to her brother.

"Yup," Ed responded. Deep in thought, he was scarcely aware of the bearded young man offering him a folder as they walked down the street.

Absent-mindedly he read the paper. ". . . New Testament inaccurate . . . Jesus a prophet, but Muhammad the greatest Prophet . . . only one complete and perfect Scripture, the holy Koran. . . . "

"Hey look, Gerry. This is a Muhammadan tract. . . . These guys are trying to convert people as they come out of a Christian church. What a nerve!"

Thus two young people from Iowa, visiting in New York, began to learn about another great "religion of the Book." They would not have had to go far to learn more. A few blocks away they could have found thousands of Black Muslims, Negroes professing their peculiar race-centered version of "Islam." In Iowa it is scarcely an hour's drive from their home in Central City to Cedar Rapids. There they could visit a large mosque with an active program of worship, missionary work and publication.

7 Islam

IN THE seventh century Islam exploded against Christendom and almost wiped it off the map. In the twentieth century that challenge is being renewed, with the destiny of whole continents hanging in the balance.

THE EARLY STORY OF ISLAM

Nearly six hundred years had come and gone since Jesus of Nazareth lived and died in Palestine. The church he founded had spread all around the Mediterranean world and far beyond. But the great arid peninsula that is called Arabia remained much as it had always been. At Mecca, one of its chief cities, the worst of Arabian paganism flourished. A black meteorite built into a corner of the temple called the Kaaba was worshiped along with other objects of stone, wood, and metal—symbols of a multitude of gods, goddesses, spirits, and forces.

To Mecca came most of the tribes of Arabia, for it was a great pilgrimage center. In the crowded bazaars drunkenness and gambling erupted on every side. Blood feuds from the back country broke out like heat lightning. Polygamy, concubinage, promiscuity were the order of the day. Unwanted baby girls were buried alive.

In this murky air there were also some disturbing ideas. From the south and east came reports of Zoroaster's religion, stressing honesty and loyalty to the Good God in his fight against Evil. Ideas were also pouring in from cities of Syria, Mesopotamia, and Arabia itself where colonies of Jews lived, telling their stories from the Hebrew Bible. In the deserts of the region were Christian monks and hermits. Many of the slaves in the bazaars were Christian captives. In Arabian paganism itself was the notion of "The God," Allah, who in some half-understood way was recognized as creator of the whole world.

Here was an explosive mixture, waiting for a spark to ignite it. In an uneasy blend were Arab disunity and poverty, the presence of religious systems higher than the prevailing paganism, and the need for a better law of life than the old Arab code could supply. One flash of genius would be enough. Almost exactly six hundred years after the time of Jesus that genius appeared.

His name was Muhammad. Since his time, more boy babies have been given that name than any other in all the history of mankind. Born in A.D. 570, he became an orphan at the age of six. In his early twenties, he became caravan manager for Khadijah, a wealthy widow, and traveled to the richer world outside Arabia.

He traveled less, however, as Khadijah fell in love with him and he, apparently, with her, even though she was years older than he. They married. His new economic security brought him leisure to pursue the religious questions which had been troubling him. For days at a time he meditated alone in a cave.

One night, called by Muslims "The Night of Power and Excellence," an overwhelming figure appeared before him. Muhammad describes the experience in Sura (chapter) 53 of the Koran. He saw "one terrible in power" standing in the highest part of the horizon, who came nearer until he stood within two bows' length and then spoke these words:

> Read: In the name of the Lord who createth,
> Createth man from a clot.
> Read: And thy Lord is the Most Bounteous,
> Who teacheth by the pen,
> Teacheth man that which he knew not.[1]

Impressive as it was, the experience was terribly upsetting. He hurried home to share his feelings with Khadijah. She assured him of her absolute faith. But for a time no more visions came, and Muhammad was tempted to despair. Then he heard again a voice from heaven, saw the angel of the first revelation seated upon a throne between heaven and earth, and heard him say, "O Muhammad, thou art the Prophet of the Lord, in truth, and I am Gabriel." After this he was reassured of his mission, and revelations began to come more frequently.

These things occurred in A.D. 610. For three years he spoke of his revelations only in private. Then he began public preaching, but after four years of jeers and persecution he could count only forty followers, including wives and slaves of believers. His wife, who had been his first and strongest supporter, died. The situation became desperate.

Almost miraculously, a delegation appeared from the city of Yathrib, three hundred miles to the north. They wished him to come and rule over their town, which was racked with disorder and bloody feuds. In 622, after a narrow escape from Mecca, Muhammad made his *hijrah* (withdrawal) to Yathrib, now called Medina, City of the Prophet. From this event the Muslim calendar dates all subsequent events—labeling them A.H. ("from the year of the *hijrah*").

At Medina, Muhammad quickly organized his new faith. He called his followers Muslims, or submitters, meaning those who submit themselves in absolute obedience to God. The faith itself he called Islam from the same Arabic root. It was above all a religion of absolute, steady obedience to the divine will. He erected a mosque for worship, instituted prayer rituals, decreed the giving of alms, and set up basic Muslim rules.

Muhammad was eminently successful. A war with Mecca turned out in his favor, and in 630 he marched triumphantly into his native city. From this point on he directed all Muslims to turn toward Mecca when they bow in prayer. He cleansed the Kaaba of its idols and ordered a purified worship at the Black Stone and the sacred well. Next he set out to unify all Arabia, by his message if possible, by force if necessary. Before his sudden death in 632, unification was well on the way.

112

THE EXPANSION OF ISLAM

Under Muhammad's three able successors as head of the Muslim religious and political community, the new faith spread like wildfire. The first caliph or successor, Abu Bakr, gave it a Scripture by having the Prophet's revelations collected into the Koran. He also mounted a military assault on the world outside Arabia. He and the two caliphs who followed presided over the conquest of Syria, Mesopotamia, Armenia, Persia, Egypt, and Cyrenaica within thirty years! Arab armies carried Islam east to central Asia and west to Morocco and Spain within a century. It is probable that travelers planted the new faith as far east as the capital of China before A.D. 700.

During the next 250 years, Muslim power was consolidated and a Muslim culture built up on the basis of Greek philosophy and the older civilizations of the Near East and North Africa. It was through this Muslim culture, incidentally, that the intellectual treasures of Greek and Roman antiquity were transmitted to Europe. A second wave of expansion occurred between A.D. 1000 and A.D. 1100. Muslim domination was extended to West Africa, Asia Minor, most of central Asia, and northern India. After another pause of two hundred years, Islam thrust into the Balkans, the steppes of Russia and Siberia, the rest of India, and into Indonesia. By 1400 the Muslim world stretched in a great belt around the known earth, reaching from the equator well north into the temperate zone. Except for the loss of Spain and Sicily and some advance

113

in Africa since then, the picture remains much the same today. Between 400 and 500 million persons are members of *Dar ul Islam,* "The House of Islam," which is thus about half the size of Christendom and second largest of the world's religious communities.

MUSLIM BELIEFS

To become a Muslim one need only repeat sincerely the simple creed: *"La ilaha il' Allah, wa Muhammad Rasul Allah,"* "There is no god but Allah, and Muhammad is sent-of-Allah." Other basic Muslim beliefs are suggested in Sura 4 of the Koran: "Whoso disbelieveth in Allah and His angels and His scriptures and His messengers and the Last Day, he verily hath wandered far astray."[2] To that list only one point needs to be added, the decrees of God.

God

Muhammad knew from childhood the old Arabian belief in *al-ilah,* a vague high God who created the world. In his vivid experience this God became personal, present, overwhelmingly real, and important. As the Koran's famous "Verse of the Throne" puts it, "Allah! There is no God save Him, the Alive, the Eternal. . . . His throne includeth the heavens and the earth, and He is never weary of preserving them. He is the Sublime, the Tremendous."[3]

At the same time this great God is "nearer to him [man] than his jugular vein."[4] And the wisdom and glory of God is beautifully expressed in the "Light-verse": "Allah is the light of the heavens and the

114

earth. . . . Light upon light, Allah guideth unto His light whom He will."[5]

Many Muslim rosaries contain ninety-nine beads, to remind the worshiper of the "Beautiful Names of God." Among the most frequently cited of these are: Lord, The One, The Mighty, The Powerful, The King, The Avenger, The Dominator, The Slayer, The Provider. Other attributes are underlined in the phrase with which every devout Muslim begins a discourse: "In the Name of God, the Merciful, the Compassionate."

In one sense the center of Muhammad's gospel was an absolute focus upon the unity of God. Against Arabian polytheism and what he mistakenly believed to be the Christian's trinity of God, Mary, and Jesus, he thundered out his denunciation of the truly unpardonable sin: "Verily, God forgiveth not the giving of partners to him; other than this will he forgive whom he pleaseth; but whosoever giveth a partner to God hath conceived a monstrous lie."[6] To this day Islam finds horrible blasphemy in *shirk*—the suggestion that there is more than one God, or that Deity is more than a single all-seeing, all-hearing, all-speaking, all-knowing, all-willing, and all-powerful Being. Islam is quite ready to accept Jesus as a great prophet of God but not to associate him with God as Son. "How can He have a child, when there is for Him no consort?"

Angels

Muhammad expressed his decisive religious experience in terms familiar to himself and his hearers as an encounter with an angel, a messenger of God. Belief

WHEN FAITH MEETS FAITH

in such servants and emissaries of Allah is another foundation of Muslim belief.

Another important class of spiritual beings are the jinn, in status midway between men and angels. They are created of fire instead of earth, and among them are both believers and infidels, good and bad.

The chief devil is Iblis or Shaytan, a fallen angel. His great sin was his refusal to worship the first man, Adam, at God's command.

Prophets

In theory, at least, Islam is extraordinarily hospitable to revelation wherever it occurs. Muslims think of Islam as simply "the religion of God." Wherever the one God truly speaks or acts, his reality is to be acknowledged. Characteristically, he makes himself known by prophets. Muhammad is last and greatest of these, but by no means the only one. Prophets have been sent to all ages and to all peoples, even to the jinn. They are not primarily miracle-workers and certainly not sharers in divinity, but really "mouthpieces" of Allah. Of the Koran's list of prophets, eighteen can be identified with individuals in the Old Testament, including Adam, Noah, Abraham, and Moses; three are mentioned in the New Testament (Zechariah, John the Baptist, and Jesus); four are Arabian; and one other seems to have part of his origin in stories about Alexander the Great! All are to be acknowledged and their messages respected without distinction.

Nevertheless, Muslims have been primarily interested in two prophets, Jesus and Muhammad. A lovely

116

Muslim custom is to add to each reference to Jesus the phrase, "blessed be he." His birth by the Virgin Mary is given Koranic authority. The New Testament, however, is considered a very badly corrupted book in which the original evangel as given by Jesus is distorted and concealed. On one critical point Muslims believe the gospels are totally wrong: Jesus was not killed by crucifixion. God took him away and substituted another figure in his place before the death on Calvary occurred. Islam has been too much impressed by the success of Muhammad to conceive that a true prophet should fail as the gospels make Jesus "fail."

But above all it is Muhammad who dominates the Muslim mind as *the* Prophet of God. He is only a man, of course, which is why one should never call his religion "Muhammadanism." No Muslim worships Muhammad. But Muslims do believe Muhammad was the greatest of men and both the most important and the last of the prophets. He is, therefore, the one whose revelation sums up all the rest and from whom the final truth is to be learned. Moreover, his life and spirit give an example for all ages. There can be no doubt that Muhammad was a magnetic and magnanimous figure, capable of inspiring great devotion, utterly sincere in his faith, a genuinely God-intoxicated man.

Scriptures

Islam, more than any other faith, is the religion of a book. But its book is no work of literature in the ordinary sense, for Muhammad could neither read nor write. Koran means "recital." It is a compilation of those messages Muhammad reported as having come directly from God and which he did not in any sense compose. He only gave voice, transmitting the words of a heavenly book that had existed from eternity with God (in Arabic!).

Muslims find the Koran incomparably great, *the* miracle of Islam which claims no miracles for its Prophet. A modern English convert calls it "that inimitable symphony, the very sound of which moves men to tears and ecstasy."[7] Both Muslims and non-Muslims, however, agree that it is a difficult book to read in translation. The original is in a poetic form intended for chanting, and there is no equivalent poetic form in Western languages. Also, it has been compiled without any logical or chronological order so that the development of thought is hard to follow in the disconnected sections. A non-Muslim, therefore, is likely to find it repetitious, murky, and confusing, highly rhetorical and over-imaginative in many parts, heavy with details of legislation, vindications of Muhammad's actions, references to problems long since outdated, and long passages of legendary lore.

Nevertheless, in Islam the Koran has the status Jesus Christ has in Christianity. It is God's Eternal Word to man, the divine source of salvation.

Judgment

Like the message of a Hebrew prophet or John the Baptist, Muhammad's original message was centered in warnings of divine judgment to come. At least 852 verses of the Koran are on that theme. The picture is painted in bold, vivid colors. The heavens will split, the mountains will be ground to dust, the graves will open, and men and jinn will be assigned to paradise or to hell.

Hell is very much to be avoided! Its inmates will be covered with fire, blown upon by pestilential winds, scalded by water, choked in black smoke, forced to eat the fruit of the tree Ez-zakkoum, which comes up from the bottom of hell and whose fruit boils up in the belly like dregs of burning oil.

But Heaven—that's another matter! Here the blessed live in gardens of delight

> On lined couches,
> Reclining therein face to face.
> There wait on them immortal youths
> With bowls and ewers and a cup from a pure
> spring
> Wherefrom they get no aching of the head nor
> any madness.

And oh, the girls!

> And (there are) fair ones with wide, lovely eyes,
> Like unto hidden pearls,
> Reward for what they used to do. . . .
> Lo! We have created them a (new) creation
> And made them virgins,
> Lovers, friends.[8]

Modern educated Muslims interpret such pictures of the rewards and punishments of the afterlife in symbolic terms. Nevertheless, according to tradition, Muhammad was particularly fond of perfume, of women, and of good food. One of the most important Muslim figures of the generation just past, King Ibn Saud of Arabia, spoke in exactly the same spirit, "Three things I have loved—perfume, women, and prayer." Passionate pursuit of fulfillment for both the senses and the spirit has marked the Muslim temper.

Divine Decrees

In the very word *Islam*, the importance of this sixth fundamental belief is underlined. Allah determines all things by his will; it is the function of man to submit to that divine determination with obedient thankfulness. Both the evil and the good that men do is done by God's decree: "Allah verily sendeth whom He will astray, and guideth whom He will."[9] It is not for us to ask the unthinkably great God, "Why?" Yet there is also a continual stress upon the justice of God. "Each soul shall be rewarded for what he has earned, and they shall not be wronged."[10] The question of divine power and justice, God's determination of all human actions and man's freedom of choice, is never really resolved. One can only note that Islam insists, far more than any other great faith, on finding in the will of God the source of all that happens.

PRACTICE OF THE MUSLIM RELIGION

From these theological puzzles, we now turn to the more practical question of how the Muslim faith is practiced. Islam is far more a way of life than a set of ideas. A Muslim's religious duties are summed up in the traditional "Five Pillars."

120

Daily Repetition of the Creed

"There is no God but Allah, and Muhammad is sent-of-Allah." This brief creed is at once the test of Muslim faith, the testimony of the convert, and the daily confession of the believer.

Prayer

It is Friday and just past noon. The high, piercing cry of the muezzin has rung out over Istanbul from one of the six pencil-thin, immensely tall minarets of the Blue Mosque. At the doorway men are taking off their shoes and checking them with the gatekeeper. Stepping inside they enter a vast hushed room under the central dome of the mosque. The entire floor is covered with rich oriental carpets. In the corners of the ceiling are Koranic verses in beautiful Arabic script, but there is no other religious symbol except a small empty niche in the front wall, the *qiblah*. Near the center of the room is a raised platform with two men on it. The worshipers sit or kneel in silence. Amid the beauty of this house of worship, the air seems charged with prayer.

Suddenly the *kari* on the platform begins to chant in Arabic. His high, beautifully modulated voice rises and falls with the cadence of the Koran's poetry, spinning a thread of unearthly verbal music. The chanting continues for minutes, while other worshipers gather. Then an impressive figure in long robe and maroon-trimmed white turban strides alongside the wall and down to the front. The worshipers rise and

121

go forward, forming a long row behind the imam or priest, who stands before the central niche, facing Mecca. The chanting stops and the prayers begin.

In perfect unison the worshipers follow the imam's lead as he utters a phrase now and then to guide them. Each one is repeating the prescribed prayers silently to himself while together they perform the ritual *rak'ah* (bowings). A sermon by the imam follows. In all the world there are few services of worship so charged with the presence of deity—and so surrounded by beauty. Muslim religious architecture from Spain to Calcutta is notable for simplicity and restraint of design, coupled with perfection of form and loveliness of decoration.

Devout Muslims through the centuries have performed a service of prayer like this individually, no less than five times a day. Even in some modern cities one may see the faithful spread out their prayer rugs wherever they may be when the time for prayer comes—dawn, midday, midafternoon, sunset, fall of darkness—and perform the bowings, facing toward Mecca and repeating Sura 1 of the Koran, the Muslim "Lord's Prayer":

Praise be to Allah, Lord of the Worlds,
The Beneficent, the Merciful.
Owner of the Day of Judgment,
Thee (alone) we worship; Thee (alone) we ask for help.
Show us the straight path,
The path of those whom Thou hast favoured;
Not (the path) of those who earn Thine anger nor of those who go astray.

Although there are variations in its application, the basic Muslim principle of the equality of all believers means that the imam is not a priest in the sense of standing between God and the people. Even the caliphs were no different in theological status than any ordinary Muslim. Here is a question well worth pondering: Could the fact that in Islam religious leaders are all laymen account in large part for its missionary success?

Almsgiving

Muhammad strengthened his brotherhood of Muslims by a process of sharing. The traditional obligation of *zakat* or alms was a share of one's annual income (some say one-fortieth), plus a proportion of one's capital wealth. This revenue provided for the religious establishment and also for a social security and general relief fund.

Fasting

During the ninth month, Ramadan, abstinence from all food and drink is required from the first brightening of the sky at dawn to the moment the sun's disk disappears at evening. In the night there are no restrictions, so that for the wealthy the fast may involve little more than rearranging one's daily schedule and going thirsty through a long day. That day may or may not be hot since, like other Muslim festivals, Ramadan moves through the year. This is because the Muslim year, based on twelve lunar months, is about eleven days shorter than our solar year.

WHEN FAITH MEETS FAITH

Pilgrimage

Every Muslim is required once in his lifetime to make a hadj, a pilgrimage to Mecca, if he can. The aim is to be there during the sacred month Zu'lhijyan, when perhaps half a million pilgrims from all over the world gather for the rituals prescribed by tradition. All must wear the same kind of seamless white garment, practice abstinence from food and drink by day, and maintain continence. The ritual actions required are strenuous and demanding, especially under the burning Meccan sun. The result is an impressive leveling and unifying experience for Muslims of every class, race, and nation.

THE CODE OF ISLAM

For Islam the burning question has not been "What is God like?" so much as "What does God command?". Muslim religious thought has focused on right action more than right belief. Muhammad founded a community that was both religious and political. In this sense Islam is totalitarian. At its heart is a comprehensive law that, like the law of Judaism, attempts to prescribe even minute details of life both for individuals and for society as a whole. The queen of Muslim studies, then, is *sharia,* Islam's code of conduct.

Parts of the Muslim code are unique. For example, there is an absolute prohibition of the use of alcohol. As a result Coca-Cola is an extremely popular drink in the Middle East! The Koran permits relatively easy divorce to men, none to women, in line with its general principle that "the men are a step above them."[11] It also permits a maximum of four wives at a time. Muslim theologians, however, are now saying that the command to treat all wives exactly alike deliberately asks the impossible and is really a prohibition of polygamy under the guise of permitting it.

In many ways Islamic law is quite similar to passages in the Hebrew and Christian Bibles. Most of the Ten Commandments find their parallels in the Koran. If one compares the Great Commandment of the New Testament with Islamic ethics, he finds significant parallels and some differences. Certainly, "You shall love the Lord your God with all your heart, soul, mind, and strength" is at the heart of Islam. "You shall love your neighbor as yourself" is harder to find, however. Even though there is much about generosity, kindness, and forgiveness, retaliation is often prescribed.[12]

This contrast with the New Testament underlines a fundamental difference between Islam and Christianity. Islam tries to give order and meaning to all human life, public and private, by means of a vast code of rules that issue from the will of an all-powerful God. Christianity believes that the quality of a person's existence can be transformed by faith in an all-loving God and that from this new kind of person a free, loving response will flow to those around him.

THE TRADITION OF PERSONAL DEVOTION

It would be quite wrong to leave the impression that Islam is all legalism. Like every great religion, it is a whole family of faiths, with differing emphases re-

125

flecting the experiences and concerns of all kinds of sincere and aspiring people touched by God in many different ways.

As Christianity has its denominations, so Islam has its numerous sects. There are the Sunnis, followers of orthodox tradition but themselves divided according to four great schools of interpretation of the Koran and Muslim law. Persia and India have millions of Shiites, who are as much devoted to Ali, the ill-starred fourth caliph, and his descendants as they are to Muhammad. Their passionate celebrations of the massacre that ended the life and the line of Husain, Ali's son, bring a note of tragedy and a depth of feeling into Islam somewhat akin to the Passion theme in Christian faith.

Most dynamic, perhaps, of the great sects of Islam is the Sufi movement. In Sufism the common man's and woman's heart takes precedence over the scholar's and the lawyer's head. Sufism has found expression in a thousand ways—in close-knit brotherhoods of worship and study, in the extravagant devotions of whirling dervishes or the flagellants, in the adoration of saints, and pilgrimages to holy places. Above all one catches the heartbeat of Sufi Islam in the marvelous devotional poetry that it has produced. For Sufism true Islam is *haqiqa*—a personal, inward grasp of the Divine Being and his will for men. Sufis love the tradition that reports God as saying: "In no way does My servant so draw nigh unto Me as when he performs those duties which I have imposed on him; and My servant continues to draw near to Me through works of supererogation, until I love him. And when I love him, I am his eye, so that he sees by Me, and his ear, so that he hears by Me, and his tongue, so that he speaks by Me, and his hand, so that he takes by Me."[13]

Rabi'a, the woman saint of the eighth century, prayed: "O God, if I worship Thee in fear of Hell, burn me in Hell, and if I worship Thee in hope of Paradise, exclude me from Paradise. But if I worship Thee for Thine own sake, withhold not Thine everlasting beauty."[14]

In this conviction that at the heart of reality there is the transcendent beauty of God, and in the passionate quest of that beauty, a Christian must recognize a spirit akin to that of his own faith. It is worth pondering the fact that Muhammad was highly responsive to much of Christian teaching as he understood it through very indirect sources. Had there been so much as an Arabic translation of the Bible, Islam might have become a Christian sect rather than a separate and sometimes hostile religion. Muhammad's break with Christians and Jews was initiated by them, not by him. What a tremendous difference to the religious history of the world it might have made had the Christian church of the sixth and seventh centuries been intelligently missionary, able to present its gospel persuasively to the young Arabian camel-driver who passed along its fringes and went on to found the strongest of its rival faiths!

Faith Meets Faith ✝ Tim seldom watches educational TV. In fact, he seldom watches TV at all, what with the pressures of homework, tennis team, cello practice, and the electronics lab he keeps going under the name of "hi fi." But when he noticed in the paper that there was to be a documentary on Red China, he decided to pick up some information for his current history class.

That evening he saw modern China. There were young people laughing, talking, pulling heavy loads of earth. They had committed themselves for three months to a great dam-building project. There were smiling youngsters in a model nursery school, playing under the watchful eyes of attractive young teachers. There were hundreds of thousands of faces massed in Peking, looking with intense devotion toward the reviewing stand on which stood Mao Tse-tung, leader of Red China. There was the strong, intelligent face of Premier Chou En-lai, responding with cool assurance to the interviewer's questions.

As he turned off the set, Tim grew thoughtful. Something powerful had gripped 600 million Chinese and set them on the march. They looked as if they knew where they were going, and seemed to believe utterly in what they were doing. Did he and his friends have what it takes to match their energy and devotion?

8 Communism

WORLD-WIDE communism represents a challenge to the very existence of Christianity as an organized community on this planet. But how does the encounter with communism come into this study of faith meeting faith?

Communism is notoriously atheistic. Karl Marx, founder of communism, declared that "religion is the opiate of the people," not only false but positively harmful. It is a drug that makes people dream about a blessed hereafter instead of fighting against evil and working toward a better society here and now. After the Communists conquered North China in the spring of 1949, they organized a *ta k'e* (big class) in each university to give the students fundamental indoctrination. And the first session of *ta k'e* started off to refute Genesis. The theme of the lectures was "Who created the world?" The answer: "Labor created the world." God had nothing to do with it. Man's intelligent effort is the source of all value.

But the antireligious look of communism is only a

disguise. Like Islam, this is a fighting faith that sprang from a biblical background. Marx was of Jewish descent, although his father had become a Christian for social reasons. In his anger against social injustice, Marx sounds very much like a nineteenth century successor of the Hebrew prophets. His great book, *Capital* (often known under its German title, *Das Kapital*), is heavy, dry economics for the most part. It comes alive, however, when Marx begins to describe such a situation as he found in the English straw-hat industry of his day:

The children commence their instruction in straw-plaiting generally in their 4th, often between their 3rd and 4th year. Education, of course, they get none. . . . They are kept at work simply to get through the task, generally 30 yards daily, prescribed by their half-starved mothers. These same mothers often make them work at home, after school is over, till 10, 11 and 12 o'clock at night. The straw cuts their mouths, with which they constantly moisten it, and their fingers. [In some "schools" there is, per child,] less space than the half of what a child would occupy if packed in a box measuring 3 feet in each direction. Thus do the children enjoy life until the age of 12 or 14. The wretched half-starved parents think of nothing but getting as much as possible out of their children. . . . It is no wonder that ignorance and vice abound in a population so brought up. . . . A great number of the women have illegitimate children, and that at such an immature age that even those most conversant with criminal statistics are astounded.

Marx adds his bitter comment: "And the native land of these model families is the pattern Christian country of Europe!"[1]

130

MARKS OF COMMUNIST RELIGION

Not only in general spirit but in many specific ways, communism reveals that it is one of the rival faiths of our time. Consider the following aspects of this crusading movement:

Scriptures

Communists, like Jews, Christians, and Muslims, are "people of a book." Though their "Bible" is not bound in a single volume, its basic writings are cited with the utmost reverence. Long sermons and applications are drawn from even casual references in them, and they are held to be the chief source of wisdom for all human problems.

Communism's "four evangelists" and some of their chief works are:

Karl Marx—*Capital, Class Struggles in France, The Communist Manifesto, The German Ideology,* (last two with Engels)

Friedrich Engels—*Anti-Dühring, The Holy Family* (with Marx)

Nicolai Lenin—*Materialism and Empirico-Criticism, The State and Revolution*

Mao Tse-tung—*On Practice, China's New Democracy, On Guerrilla Warfare*

A few years ago the fourth evangelist would have been Joseph Stalin, Soviet dictator from 1927 until his death in 1953, but a violent campaign has debunked him and the Chinese version of communism has come into greater prominence.

WHEN FAITH MEETS FAITH

Theology

Upon these "scriptures" rests a highly developed system of communist doctrine. Its general name is "dialectical materialism," a term that points both to communism's view of how the world works and to its conviction about the "Lord" of this world and its history.

Communists begin with the assertion that reality is fundamentally material. Marx's phrase is, "Consciousness does not determine life, but life determines consciousness." Physical facts come before mental facts; geology and biology before psychology. Mental facts—ideas, attitudes, motives—do not create physical or material situations; they only reflect them.

The most important material facts, the doctrine continues, are property and the way in which goods are produced and distributed. Communism sees history moving restlessly from one stage to another, driven and directed by changing forms of economic life. In this connection it makes use of Hegelian thought. In the early nineteenth century, the German philosopher Hegel popularized the idea of dialectic. Hegel, an idealist, said that one idea, which he called "thesis," generates its opposite, "antithesis," and in turn the antithesis generates a third idea, the "synthesis" or higher stage beyond the thesis and antithesis. (To illustrate: *puritanism* with its repression of natural impulses, leads to *license* and loss of moral discipline; which in turn gives way to a *morality* providing for the normal and creative expression of impulses within the framework of a proper discipline.)

132

Marx said that he stood Hegel on his head. He kept the idea of dialectic, but he saw it operating through economic and other material pressures, not moral and spiritual forces. Thus, at the beginning of European history, the production and distribution of goods was organized in a system called feudalism. Society was dominated by landholders who kept the common people bound to the soil or to traditional local handicrafts. Feudalism provided a certain degree of social order and was productive enough to keep the population alive. But it was rigid and unprogressive and created more and more dissatisfaction, especially among the new merchant and banking class that began to grow strong at the end of the Middle Ages. This new business class, the *bourgeoisie*, then took over society through a series of revolutions and created a system of free private enterprise called capitalism. In the nineteenth century, Europe was dominated by this capitalist antithesis to feudalism. The capitalist system produced a very active, productive, prosperous society. It also created something else, an enormous class of oppressed laborers whose work produced vast wealth but who received only enough to keep themselves alive. The profits from their labor were stolen by the capitalists who ran the system. Remember Marx's description of the straw-hat industry and the kind of labor upon which it depended?

By exploiting this huge group of workers or "proletarians," says communist doctrine, capitalism is digging its own grave. For the laborers are bound to rebel, and in their rebellion the whole system will be shaken to the ground. Then a new synthesis will arise, a classless society in which the proletariat will dominate. So *The Communist Manifesto* concludes that the way ahead can only be cleared "by the forcible overthrow of the whole extant social order. Let the ruling classes tremble at the prospect of a communist revolution. Proletarians have nothing to lose but their chains. They have a world to win."[2]

This may sound like a theory about how history operates, but it is really a description of the communist "Almighty." Says Marx, "What the bourgeoisie therefore produces, above all, are its own grave-diggers. Its fall and the victory of the proletariat are equally inevitable."[3] The dialectic that shoves history forward, irresistibly, toward higher and higher stages, is the creator and savior of mankind. By this dialectical process, our lives are shaped and ruled. In the end it will bring us to our eternal home, the kingdom of man. Many of the functions that God performs in the theistic religions are performed in communism by the dialectic.

Just as Christianity and Judaism have their Messiah, a chosen individual through whom God works, so communism has its instrument through whom the dialectic works. Each new age is produced when an older ruling class is overthrown by a new and rising one. The feudal lords were eliminated by middle-class merchants, bankers, and manufacturers. Now the capitalist society is to be overthrown by the pent-up power of an oppressed laboring class. Thus, in our age the workers of the world make up a messianic class.

This communist "theology" also has a distinct and important viewpoint on man. From one angle, communism makes man virtually divine. His intelligence and his productive labor are the highest realities in the universe, for there is no God. All hope for the future arises from the efforts of the working class to destroy the capitalist system and to create a new society with justice and plenty for all. This is a religion of humanism—reverence for human abilities, faith in human effort.

On the other hand, communism's man is a curiously stunted being. The functioning of his mind is just a product of his economic situation. He thinks what he must think, as a laborer or as a capitalist. He has no real freedom, no genuine originality. Nor does he have any real value, in and of himself. He is worth only what his class status makes him worth. Mao Tse-tung put it very clearly in his address to the Yenan Conference of Literature and Art workers in 1942:

"There is no human nature in the abstract. In a class society there is only human nature as class nature. We advocate a human nature of the . . . masses; on the other hand, the landlord class and capitalist class advocate a human nature of their own class."

Here, quite clearly, we see man crushed and flattened to the dimensions of a helpless puppet, moving his limbs and thinking his little thoughts, at the mercy of the social situation into which he has been thrust by the accident of birth or fortune. The communist man lacks even the Christian dignity of being a sinner responsible for his actions!

Ethics

Like every religion, communism teaches a code of conduct as well as a system of beliefs. We have just seen how little communism cares for man as such. The way any particular man is to be treated depends entirely upon his social relationships. There is no abstract justice to which a problem can be referred. There is only a class interest that indicates the capitalist good or the proletarian good.

Christian ethics center in the idea of love, caring for other persons as God has cared for us, but for communism this is nonsense. "Some of our comrades have been mistaken in saying that everything must start from 'Love,' " says Mao Tse-tung. "There is only *class* love in a class society."[4]

A Chinese writer who advocated human sympathy for former landlords and businessmen in their sufferings was severely criticized. "To have [that] kind of 'human feeling' . . . is actually to have no feeling for the working people, that is, to have an ambiguous attitude toward the party. . . . This shows that they have a disposition which belongs to the oppressors' class standpoint."[5] Such is the fundamental inhumanity of communism, reinforced by another of its doctrines to which we now direct our attention.

Eschatology

This term comes from the Greek word for "end," *eschaton*. It refers to the biblical teaching about the end of time and the coming of the kingdom of God.

Christians argue a good deal about exactly what this fulfillment of God's purpose means, but communists are not permitted any argument. Their expectation is clear and strong and fierce. It goes like this:

Conditions under capitalism must grow worse and worse, as the rich get richer and the poor get poorer. (This is, of course, the contrary of what has happened in twentieth century societies, but communist doctrine is not easily changed by mere facts.) Capitalist economy will totter, weakened by imperialist wars for markets and raw materials. Finally, the workers of the world will unite and overthrow capitalism. A new classless society will be set up. Governments, with their police and jails used to enforce capitalist domination, will wither away and be replaced by glad, voluntary co-operation. The economic system will operate according to the principle, "From each according to his ability, to each according to his need." There will be no grumbling about this because work will be a pleasure. The economy will be so well organized that people will spend most of their time on culture and recreation. All the imperfections in human nature caused by oppression and injustice will fade away, and for the first time true humanity in all its glory will appear.

It is a wonderful picture. Unfortunately, there is no reason to believe in it. How can class struggle produce a classless society? Why should the dialectic of history stop operating at just the point when the proletariat takes over? What will make governments wither away, when forty-five years of Russian and twelve years of Chinese Communism indicate exactly the reverse? Such is the sheer irrational faith of "scientific socialism," as Marx loved to call it.

The other difficulty with communist eschatology is that it sacrifices the present entirely to the future. If today six million Ukrainian peasants must die of starvation for the sake of the communist society of tomorrow, so be it. If 600 million Chinese must live in a virtual slave labor camp for thirty years to build the communist future, the decision is made without hesitation.

Church

Until the *eschaton* arrives, communism recognizes that a small select group of mankind is required to give spiritual and political leadership to all the rest. This faithful core of the new humanity is the Communist Party. History turned a corner in 1903 when Lenin split the communist movement and his Bolshevik group took control. His idea was that only a small, utterly dedicated, highly trained elite under iron discipline should make up the Communist Party. In other words, communism is a movement to save the masses, but the masses are not fit to belong to it, or at least to have any say in it! In actuality, the party is made up largely of intellectuals and other middle-class types (Marx, for instance, or Lenin, who came from the Russian nobility). But in some mystical way, it represents the true proletariat and leads the workers to victory. When the revolution has succeeded a "dictatorship of the proletariat"—that is, of the party—is set up. The

138

party rules all classes, including the workers, on the principle of "democratic centralism." One of the best descriptions of how this Communist "church" operates is found in the famous Grand Inquisitor scene in Dostoevsky's novel, *The Brothers Karamazov*. In that passage it is significant that the fanatical Cardinal of the Spanish Inquisition speaks also for the fanatical Communist functionary.

Conversion

To become a member of the party or its faithful follower, a radical religious experience is required. Normal personal desires are given up, and one's mind and life are totally committed to the communist cause. The Chinese phrase for it is *kai szu-hsiang*, literally "repent"! One enthusiastic young woman told how her experience in a communist labor battalion had made her a changed person. Even cleaning latrines, carrying the sewage to the fields, and spreading it carefully among the plants now seemed pleasant and glorious. "The manure no longer smells!" she reported. A very popular type of meeting in China centers in the distribution of red paper hearts to members of the audience, who are urged to put their names on them and come forward (at the "altar call") to "give their heart to the Party."

Techniques used to create this kind of personal remolding range from protracted study and indoctrination to the more violent combination of physical torture and relentless questioning and persuasion known as brainwashing.

Missions

No other movement in human history, not even Islam, has spread with such speed and power as communism. In 1916 Lenin and a handful of Bolshevik colleagues crossed Europe in a sealed railroad car and stepped out at St. Petersburg. Less than fifty years later, the revolution for which they were "the grain of mustard seed" controlled many nations, including the largest and strongest in both Europe and Asia, had a foothold in the Americas, and dominated the lives of at least one-third of mankind. Such is the result of great zeal, highly organized and backed by military power. We have described Communism as a church. It might be better to call it a missionary society.

A South African Communist describes the spirit of his mission: "Let the Christians *talk! We act!* Out of our salaries and wages we keep only what is strictly necessary, and give the rest to the cause. We give all our free time, and are ready to sacrifice anything—even our lives—for the triumph of social justice. We will win because we believe in the Communist doctrine, and Christians give only a little time and only a little money for the spreading of their Gospel. They're afraid to soil their hands!"[6]

PROSPECTS FOR COMMUNISM

What is the future of this spectacularly successful twentieth century atheistic religion? Certainly, it stands for some truths of which the world must take account. For instance:

The truth that thinking is not done in a vacuum, but that our ideas do reflect practical situations and selfish interests. Every system of thought is likely to be an "ideology," that is, a way of rationalizing special concerns and practical desires. The clash of ideas often represents a clash of power interests. Hypocrisy, to use Jesus' term, is always with us.

The truth that those who are specially poor or specially oppressed ought to have special consideration. The gospels and the prophets are full of this idea. *The Communist Manifesto* is no more radical than the Magnificat of the New Testament.

The truth that economic interests are particularly powerful in motivating individuals and groups. All of us tend to be aggressive and sensitive about anything that affects our pocketbook. In this sense we are engaged in a class struggle.

On the other hand, communism stands clearly condemned by the tyranny, the inhumanity, the brutality with which it has cursed the lives of hundreds of millions of people. It has brought some social gains to backward societies like China—better transportation, public health, education—but at a fearful price in forced labor and loss of liberty. In his novel, *1984,* George Orwell describes the demonic power drive of a Communist functionary for whom Stalin was perhaps the most obvious model:

We are priests of power. God is power. . . . The old civilizations claimed that they were founded on love and justice. Ours is founded upon hatred. . . . There will be no loyalty except loyalty toward the Party. There will be no

141

love, except the love of the Big Brother. There will be no laughter, except the laugh of triumph over a defeated enemy. All competing pleasures will be destroyed. But always . . . there will be the intoxication of power, constantly increasing and constantly growing subtler. Always, at every moment, there will be the thrill of victory, the sensation of trampling on an enemy who is helpless. If you want a picture of the future, imagine a boot stamping on a human face forever.[7]

Even worse than its physical cost is communism's spiritual cost: the destruction of free and responsible personality. Again Orwell summarizes the matter in a commissar's conversation: "Power is in tearing human minds to pieces and putting them together in new shapes of your own choosing. . . . We shall squeeze you empty, and then we shall fill you with ourselves."[8]

No better account has ever been given of what makes communism strong and of what finally makes it unbearable than the testimonies of six former Communists, all famous writers, collected in the book *The God That Failed.*[9] Why were they drawn to communism? Because of the evil and injustice of present social conditions and the vision of universal well-being that communism offered. Arthur Koestler saw in communism the only bulwark against Naziism in Germany. Ignazio Silone was driven to it by the senseless oppression of the poor in southern Italy. Richard Wright, the Negro on relief, saw in it the best hope of racial justice. André Gide found he must have some ideal to believe in but believed that Christianity had become bankrupt. He felt that if Christianity had really fulfilled the teaching of Christ, there would today be

no question of communism. Louis Fischer was capti-
vated by the universal, world-embracing vision of communism. Stephen Spender's pilgrimage to communism
began with what he had read in the gospels as a boy,
that all men are equal in the eyes of God and that the
riches of the few are an injustice to the many. He
wanted to break down the terrible conditions that separate men from one another and seal some into slums
as stifling as the tomb.

These same writers explain why it is that this "God"
finally fails. Each discovered that this movement
which promises to remedy the wrongs of the earth
leads to more wrong than the conscience can bear:
dishonesty, stupidity, arrogance, brutality, treachery,
tyranny, injustice, prostitution of art, and betrayal of
idealism. A sincere faith, directed to something other
than the true God, poisons the world. The great idol of
arrogant human idealism crushes its worshipers and
all those upon whom its shadow falls.

Faith Meets Faith ✝ Greg tossed the sports section of the *Tribune* aside. Grady Jackson was a good ball-player, sure, but how could he be so stupid. Imagine telling a reporter that he prays to his patron saint before every game and believes that this helps him to win. And then declaring that, if he loses, it is because the opposition prayed harder!

That evening, Greg had some second thoughts about Grady Jackson's church. At the university "Y" for a program on "Modern Philosophies," he learned that the new Roman Catholic chaplain would replace the announced speaker. Oh boy, Greg thought, now we're going to get it—patron saints and all. He could not have been more mistaken. Taking his bearings from the scientific philosophy of de Chardin and the existentialism of Marcel, the crew-cut young priest spun a line of thought as fine as any philosophy professor's. As the speaker showed how the teachings of his church can stand up to modern moods, Greg was puzzled. How can this be the same church that leads a man to believe that a sports score depends on whose patron saint gets the most prayers? Is it just the name that the shortstop and the chaplain have in common, or do they really belong to the same religion? How can that religion involve both superstition and lofty philosophy?

9   The Distinctiveness of My Own Faith

ONE OF the most important facts about the faiths by which men live is this: each name of a religion is a label that can be attached to many varieties of belief and practice. Even the label "Protestant" covers an enormous package. The average Presbyterian, for example, would find himself far from home among the "Protestant" snake handlers in the Tennessee mountains, the Unitarians of Boston, the Lutherans of Wisconsin, or the Baptists of Harlem. The differences would, of course, be partly a matter of culture, manners of singing and speaking, habitual ways of praying and preaching. But they would go far deeper than that. Basic concepts of how God works and how he intends man to worship and behave would be different. Most Christians now believe that their faith requires them to work for a brotherhood of men regardless of race. Yet White Citizens' Councils in the South generally base their membership upon three main requirements: white skin, belief in the divinity of Christ, and support of racial segregation!

As a Zen Buddhist professor in Japan remarked recently, "I'm sure there is something to Christianity, but Christians don't seem to know what it is!"

This does not mean that religious labels mean nothing at all. An Italian peasant woman and a Chinese Roman Catholic intellectual may both be Roman Catholics quite sincerely. They both accept the final authority of the Roman Church as embodied in the Pope and the hierarchy. What they understand that authority to mean and to teach, however, may be so vastly different as to strain the imagination. Likewise, the snake handlers and the Wisconsin Lutherans and some of the Boston Unitarians are all Protestant in two ways at least: they claim to be Christians and they reject the authority of Rome. With Roman Christians they share some kind of belief in God and some kind of loyalty to Christ. But will they agree on what kind of belief it is, in what kind of God, and what they mean by being loyal to Christ? Hardly.

Actually, the same uncertainty haunts most of the denominational labels that Protestants wear. A Methodist student is apt to find himself more at home spiritually with fellow members of the university who may be Presbyterian, Baptist, United Church, or Episcopalian, than with some of his fellow Methodists in the little Bible Belt towns of southern Illinois.

Here, then, is our starting point. To understand the real faith of the people I encounter, I must look beneath their religious labels to see what they actually believe in and live for. This goes for myself as well. I cannot determine the distinctiveness of my own faith by holding up a card marked Christian, or Protestant, or even Mennonite or Disciples of Christ. Such a label may give some useful clues. It points in certain directions and rules out some possibilities, at least, but within these very wide limits, many kinds of faith are possible.

One of the best ways to get behind the labels is to ask, "What is this kind of religion most interested in? What does it hold to be the most important reality in the world? Where does it get its clue to what life is all about?"

Or the question might be put in another way: "All religion is a matter of reverence for something or other. What is the object of greatest reverence in this particular faith?"

When one looks over the whole sweep of mankind's religious life, one finds the answers to these questions falling into four main groups. The divisions are not entirely clear, and there is some overlapping. Nevertheless, the many faiths begin to fall into a logical pattern and the basic differences among them begin to show up.

Many religions are primarily concerned about Nature. Some of these center in reverence for the natural world, its mysteries, powers, and beauties. They are really forms of Nature worship. Others are primarily intent upon getting away from Nature. They want to free men from the power of natural forces and processes. They reject all that happens in time and space, what the body does, and what comes through the senses.

On the other hand, certain religions are primarily concerned about persons. Some of these are man-centered. They believe that the highest and most dependable reality in the world is humanity. These are the humanisms. Some faiths are centered upon a person who is believed to be infinitely higher than man, perfect or nearly perfect in character, supremely powerful, everlasting, and wise, yet willing to be involved with man in a genuine personal relationship. This invisible spiritual person is called God in English, Allah in Arabic, Yahweh or Jehovah in Hebrew, *theos* in Greek. These religions are the various theisms.

NATURE-CENTERED FAITH

Each of these ways of faith has a certain appeal and a definite power. Take, for instance, the religions whose primary concern is with Nature. Beyond a question the worship of Nature expressed man's earliest religious impulse.

Reverence for Nature

As we noticed in our first chapter, the cave men of Ice Age Europe were almost certainly worshipers of Nature, especially Nature as represented in the life of animals upon whom they depended for food. In fact, most aboriginal religions belong to this family. Primitive man is very close to Nature in his way of life. He is so terribly dependent upon the rain, the sun, the seeds of plants, and an abundance of animal prey, that he can hardly help centering his prayer and trust and reverence here.

But am I, a person of the twentieth century, any less dependent upon Nature? Where does my food come from, when I look behind the facade of supermarkets? Am I any less a part of the animal kingdom than my savage ancestor, though I may ride in a powerful car and sit behind plate-glass windows in an air-conditioned building? Am I not born, do I not eat and sleep and get sick and mate and grow old and die like all other living creatures?

More than that, how can I help revering the vast process that brings spring to the dead winter world, wakens the roots hidden in the cold earth, sends the green shoot—hardly more than a slender column of water articulated in cells of inconceivable delicacy and order—up into the air and crowns it with this tiny fantasy of beauty that I call a violet? In color and form, in design and pattern, in scent and structure, there is enough wonder right here to keep me busy for a lifetime, trying to fathom and appreciate it. And Nature is infinitely rich in such miracles.

No wonder that Protestant young people, looking over a valley at vesper time, may join voices in a song of Nature worship as deep as their ancestors ever knew:

> Peace I ask of thee, O River,
> Peace, peace, peace.

Much the same experience is reflected in a Chinese painting of mountains and sea, in a fragment of Zen poetry, in the animal images at a Shinto shrine, or in the drumming and dancing of an African full-moon festival or a Hawaiian *luau*. No other form of religion is quite so sensitive in perceiving and expressing the mystic wonder of existence. None has a greater sense of reality, for what is more richly real and inescapable than Nature herself?

But faiths that center in reverence for Nature also have serious problems. For one thing, there is no discrimination in Nature. Everything that is is surely natural! And so Nature religion has no basis for judgment; no better or worse, no higher or lower, no good or evil.

Instead of Ten Commandments it has only one, "Do what comes naturally!" The genius of Nature faith is to celebrate the vitality of existence, to give full play to all the powers of our natural instincts. One of the most dramatic of these natural capacities in mankind is sexual vitality. A battle between Baal, the Nature god of virility and fertility, and Jehovah, who calls men to purity and faithfulness in sexual relations, is very important in the Old Testament—and in twentieth century America!

Nature faith not only fails at the point of moral discrimination, it actually tends to lower men to the animal level. After all, any insect or rodent is as much a part of the natural order as a human being is. If the only principle is reverence for life, then all living forms are equally worthy of protection and respect. This is why some kinds of Indian religion set so much store by the indiscriminate protection of all life. If

rats eat the food that would save starving babies—
well, they are living beings, too. As John Steinbeck
makes clear in his novel, *Cannery Row,* an invocation
addressed to the God of Nature would have to bless him
for having given the power of survival equally to the
gopher, the mosquito, the brown rat, and man. This is
precisely why a second cluster of faiths arose, in sharp
opposition to Nature worship in all its forms.

Rejection of Nature

Because Nature worship fails to discriminate between better and worse, higher and lower, some persons go to the opposite extreme. They reject Nature
entirely, even human nature. They say, "This is all de-
lusion, all sham. Nothing is real except spirit. Nothing is worth loving or fearing or respecting except your
own inmost self. Everything else is only passing, only
deceptive appearance. Get rid of it all—and set yourself free."

Buddha's life portrays this fight against Nature. He
cut every desire for things in the world of space and
time, even for his own existence. And when this desirelessness was accomplished, he was in nirvana, in
which nothing natural had any power over him whatever.

This path has been recommended by many. Early
Christian hermits who fled to the desert or walled
themselves up in caves illustrate this religion of anti-
Nature. Many mystical philosophers suggest the same
thing: that true reality and true value are to be found
only in a realm of pure ideas, far removed from the

physical world. Classic Hinduism identifies the inmost self, atman, with the universal reality, Brahman. It denies that there is anything else but these two-in-one, which are pure spirit. This is another way of expressing the religion of anti-Nature.

Such a faith, under any label, represents a tremendous effort of the human spirit. Here is a really athletic religiousness fighting against all the forces that try to make us conform to the natural world around us and within us.

On the other hand, there is something pathetic about such faith. A creed that tries to blind my eyes to the beauty of the starry universe and calls it only a shimmer of unreal forces, that bids me stop all loving, all caring, all friendship, is a tragic thing. Moreover, it is hard to take it seriously. Somehow, the reality of my own existence, the importance of at least a few other persons, and some joy in the splendid pageant of nature, almost inevitably force themselves upon my consciousness.

Perhaps it is not too much to say that the religions of anti-Nature are self-contradictory. It is virtually impossible for anyone to live by them. Their strength lies in their protest against what is wrong with Nature worship. Yet even the protest has its dangers. It easily generates a passive, don't-care attitude toward the problems and possibilities of existence. To be concerned for a better life, either for oneself or for others, is to commit a spiritual error. This only pulls tighter the chains of concern. Cultures affected by this religious aversion to everything natural have been stagnant.

Moreover, they have often been easy prey to those who took the natural desires for power and wealth only too seriously.

PERSON-CENTERED FAITH

Thus neither of the great ways of faith focused upon Nature seems to be adequate. One of them subordinates man to subhuman and impersonal Nature, the other cuts off his proper vitality and drains away the reality of existence. No wonder that throughout history there have been many who declared this whole preoccupation with Nature, either to worship it or reject it, to be a fundamental mistake. These people have been drawn to personality as the ultimate focus of faith.

Reverence for Man

Among those who stress personality are the humanists. They have said, "The proper study of man is man." It is humanity itself, with its wonderful capacities, to which reverence ought to be directed. One applicant for missionary service wrote on his application papers, "My religion consists in reverence for human experience." Such is the age-old creed of the humanistic faiths.

Some humanistic religions have centered upon the individual human being and his innate possibilities. The ancient philosopher Epicurus advised his followers to "cultivate your garden." That is, make the very most of whatever abilities and opportunities you have to enjoy life. Explore all the possibilities of hu-

153

man experience, nurture every flower of physical and mental and moral excellence that your life can produce. True, your powers are limited. Fate may wound you and death will surely come. But if you make the most of the possibilities within your grasp you will have come as near salvation as any human being can. You will have manifested the peculiar excellence of being human, and there is no other excellence as high as that.

In our own century the American philosopher John Dewey summarized what he called a "common faith" by calling for reverence toward human values.

Ours is the responsibility of conserving, transmitting, rectifying and expanding the heritage of values we have received that those who come after us may receive it more solid and secure, more widely accessible and more generously shared than we have received it. Here are all the elements for a religious faith that shall not be confined to sect, class, or race.[1]

Much traditional humanism was individualistic. It concentrated upon what the single human being could accomplish. It taught him to put his faith in his own powers. But it has become clear—if, indeed, there ever was any doubt about it—that on the whole the individual human is a puny and inglorious being. Hardly a fit object of religious devotion! Indeed, to make of oneself a god seems to be the surest way of turning into a monster. Leopold and Loeb, the two brilliant young Chicago students who coolly murdered a boy to demonstrate that they were above all moral law, reminded the world of this fact. Such is the result when men try to act like God and pretend that they, and not a higher law, are the measure of all things.

In our time, therefore, the humanistic faiths have tended to shift from an individualistic to a social form. Not myself but my class, my nation, my party, my race—these collectives become gods. Can we remember

—the German *Volk* and the religion of Naziism?
—the Jets, the teen-age gang in *West Side Story*?
—the American who said, "Our country, right or wrong!"?
—the ultra-Zionism for which a group of Jewish terrorists did their bloody work?
—the Communist Party and the religion of communism?

An unforgettable array of religions, truly. Probably no worse collection has ever existed in all human history. Why are they so bad? Why do faiths that begin with reverence for human values become so monstrous? One remembers the stories in Genesis about the desire of men to become like God, to learn the secrets of good and evil, and to build a tower reaching to heaven. Perhaps Genesis is right in suggesting that the original sin, most fundamental and ravaging of all, is for man to confuse himself with God.

But this is to get ahead of our story or, rather, to lead us to its final chapter. We have examined in turn three of the four great ways of faith that men have followed. Two were preoccupied with Nature—one worshiping it, one denying it. The third was preoccupied with man himself. What other possibility is there?

155

WHEN FAITH MEETS FAITH

Reverence for God

There has occurred to men over and over again, in many times and places, the notion that the highest and most important reality is not Nature but a Person, not a limited person like man but an infinite person within whose purpose the whole universe exists and to whom man can be related not only as a creature but as a son.

To a considerable extent belief in one God has had to be carried through the world by the missionaries of Judaism, Christianity, and Islam. The idea of a Being who is most real and most powerful, who yet cannot be seen or touched or tested in any ordinary way, is a difficult one. Nevertheless, the idea that a single God rules the universe keeps cropping up in all sorts of places. African animists, spirit-and-nature worshipers, have dimly known a high God. Confucius sometimes spoke as if he trusted him; and the remarkable Chinese teacher Mo-ti developed a theology very much like that of the Hebrew prophets. The Buddhas and bodhisattvas of Mahayana Buddhism and the gods of Hinduism sometimes look remarkably like the God of theistic faith. All in all, there is enough reverence for God scattered over the earth to make one believe there must be reality behind the forms. Otherwise, how could so improbable an idea have arisen so often and in so many places?

The distinctiveness of God-centered faith and its remarkable values become clear as soon as we begin seriously to compare it with the other three. In such faith Nature receives its full due. It is God's creation, and

God is continually revealing himself through it. "This is my Father's world," so I reverence and enjoy it to the full. But because God is Spirit and because he made man in his own image, I am able to discriminate between lower and higher, good and better, and to give priority to personal and spiritual values.

Man also receives his full due. He is no longer just another natural fact. He has a special divine meaning. He is a unique channel for God's creating, saving, and revealing activity, and he is responsible for developing those powers in himself that are most like God's. Yet, while recognizing himself to be made in God's image, man is defended against the terrible temptation to worship himself. For he is made by God, dependent upon God, and intended to live to the glory of God. In a wonderful way, God-centered faith thus conserves the real values of the humanisms, the Nature religions, and even the faiths that try to master Nature by rejecting it completely.

But faith in God, obviously, is not a single religion. I must recognize that the term "God" can bear very different meanings.

Judaism portrays God as the source of order, as fundamentally a lawgiver. In the Gospels we see Jesus rejected by Jewish leaders for what they took to be his contempt for God's Law. In the book of Acts, Christianity emerged as a new religion, separated from Judaism by its welcome to people of races who neither knew nor kept the ritual law. Against this openness, Judaism resolutely turned its back.

Historic Judaism is, of course, not the only place

157

where one may see faith in God as primarily a law-giver. Many Christians give evidence of believing that God is terribly concerned about the keeping of rules and the observance of rituals. This tendency is even more marked in much of Islam. Yet the real emphasis in Islam is generally somewhere else. It is not so much the law of God as the sheer and overwhelming power of God that has been central in the history of Muhammad's people. The Muslim, as we have seen, is a submitter who bows before the divine majesty in total humility and reverence.

Such stress upon the power of God is not confined to Islam. Among Christian theologians many have so emphasized God's sovereignty that they left little room for human choice or responsibility. God is described as arbitrarily assigning some of his creatures to salvation, others to eternal torment, long before they come into existence. Here, as in much Muslim theology, one looks in vain for any clear indication of the character of God by which his vast power is directed.

Surely, that is a long way from the heart of the biblical faith. In the Bible it is neither God as lawgiver nor God as power whom we see most clearly. The First Letter of John sums up the matter: "God is love." In the cross the church has seen that "God so loves the world that he gave his only Son," has seen a love that is deeper and stronger than anything else in the world. "I am sure that neither death, nor life, nor angels, nor principalities . . . nor anything else in all creation, will be able to separate us from the love of God. . . ."[2] It is the love of God that focuses the worship of Chris-

158

tians, calls forth their faith, and awakens their answering love.

This, then, is the distinctiveness of the faith held by one who seeks to follow Jesus: that God is really to be known in terms of love. A simple point? Obvious? Perhaps. Yet, looking at the panorama of Christian faith, one wonders. The dominant school of Roman Catholic theology interprets God as Being rather than as Love. It is his sheer existence, his self-contained eternity, that gets most attention. As we have noted, there are other Christian theologies that really put the divine law or divine power above the divine love.

The fact is that this simplest statement of the gospel is the most profound. Perhaps it is also the most difficult, because it calls upon a Christian to express his faith through love, an unlimited and undefeated love like God's. Nowhere else in all the wonderful array of the faiths of men do we see so clearly that we live within the purpose and under the command of a God whose whole nature is love. Nowhere does that fact come with such power and certainty as it does in him from whom Christians take their name. Here is the true distinctiveness of their faith.

Faith Meets Faith ✝ Forty young people from overseas countries came to the United States for three months under the auspices of a leading metropolitan newspaper. They lived in American homes, attended American schools, and talked with new-found friends from every continent. They found the experience highly rewarding—and upsetting.

Their religious ideas in particular were shaken by exposure to a new situation and to the different ideas of others. One Indian girl from a Hindu family background said, "I have been disillusioned completely, to the extent of questioning everything that I have been taught." A Protestant from Britain felt he had to break completely with organized religion. Knowing how this would hurt his family, he raised the defiant and probing question, "Should you let respect for your mother come between you and a search for the truth?"[1]

10 Called to Witness

IN THIS book we have been having an encounter. At least in imagination, we have come face to face with the fact that the world has many great religions, not just one, and that each tells its own persuasive story about the truth of things.

We all face the question, "Should respect for our parents or our minister or fear of what others would think stand between us and a search for the truth?" Of course not. If faith consisted of burying one's head in the sand, the ostrich might be its symbol. Can you see it, a stained glass window featuring that great wingless bird coyly hiding its eyes in a convenient gopher hole? Hardly! The seal of the World Council of Churches has a ship with a mast in the form of a cross. Exploration and adventure, risk on an uncharted ocean, are what the ship calls for. And the cross—nothing ever got closer to hard fact than the cross, and no one ever put truth more clearly above tradition than the man who died on it. For a Christian there is no other way to handle an explosive encounter with other faiths than to face their beliefs and the questions they raise squarely and fairly.

In such encounter, there are four positions one can take about faiths other than his own.

THE CLOSED-MIND POSITION

"My faith is right; all others are wrong." This is a very clear and simple attitude. It is popular among simple people who do not like to be confused by having to deal with complicated facts. Unfortunately, it leads to all kinds of absurdities. An American missionary in Turkey overheard a conversation in a coffee house one day. The local druggist was talking with some cronies about the town's missionary doctor. "Yes, I know Dr. Nute is an infidel and is going to burn forever in hell after he dies," said the druggist in a loud voice. "But I'll tell you one thing. If I get sick I want *him* to be my doctor and nobody else!"

As a good Muslim, the druggist felt compelled to believe that the Christian doctor's religion was all wrong, so utterly wrong that he would be tortured forever for holding to it. At the same time, he recognized that this utterly wrong religion had impelled the American to leave his comfortable home and travel far across the seas to set up practice in his town, and had made him a person of such integrity and loving skill that one would gladly entrust his life to him. How could a religion that is all wrong have such wonderful effects?

Moreover, other faiths cannot be completely wrong because they have so much in common with one another. Muslims, Christians, and Jews, as we have

162

seen, share a common basic faith in one God, creator and companion of mankind. They believe in his justice and power and mercy—although perhaps in different ways and with different emphases. With Buddhists, Christians share a conviction that the spirit is more important than the body. With Hindus, they agree that the body has its own proper importance, too. The simple theory that my religion is so utterly different from all others that it can be totally right, and all others totally wrong, simply does not fit the facts confronted when faith meets faith.

THE OPEN-MINDED ATTITUDE

Swinging to the other extreme, many people take the position, "All religions are really right." They may explain their statement by adding, "Fundamentally, and in their best expressions, all religions affirm the same great truths. Different names are only labels. They point to differences in custom and tradition, but these lie only on the surface. Ultimately, all faiths lead to God."

This is probably, in some form, the most popular view among thinking people today, and it is worth some very careful examination. A Roman Catholic priest calls for the world's religions to reach a "summit agreement" so that they can present "a united front."[2] A great philosopher says that the real truth of religion is already present in each faith, at least in principle: "The several universal religions are already fused together, so to speak, at the top."[3] The coach of a championship professional football team believes in the value of faith, any faith. "It doesn't matter where you go to church. The important thing is to have religion."[4]

It is true that the great religions do have some things in common: they provide certain similar benefits to their followers. One observer says that in Southeast Asia, Buddhism tends to produce such things as personal peace of mind, moral standards for society, a sense of human dignity, support for the national life and aspiration of the people, a sense of mission in the world, an appreciation of beauty, and opportunities for community fun and fellowship.[5] Much the same could be said of Christianity in its many forms, of Islam, of Hinduism, or of Judaism.

In another way, the radical mystics of one religion tend to speak like those of all others. They testify that their individual personality is merging with a vast spiritual reality. Their language about the divine tends to be that of lover and beloved who find fulfillment in union. Or again, the philosophers of Hinduism, of Islam, of Christianity, sound surprisingly alike. They tend to analyze reality in similar ways and to find a divine creative reason akin to the mind of man at work in the universe.

Nevertheless, by now we should be perfectly clear how different the major faiths of mankind really are. Some center in a personal God; others deny such a God. Some find the soul of man to be the ultimate reality; others deny that the soul exists. Even where God is worshiped, he is conceived in such different ways that he seems, in different times and different places, to be a different God. With all their similarities, the great faiths have sharp and irreconcilable differences. One may choose one or the other, but he cannot choose them all unless he is willing to believe contradictory things. If it is true that God is love, as Jesus' cross declares, then it cannot be true that God is more concerned for justice than for anything else or that he really wants blind obedience on man's part.

On investigation, the idea that all religions are equally right turns out to mean that they are also equally wrong. Each has some of the truth, but none has the whole truth; therefore, some degree of inadequacy, if not of actual error, is present in every one. On this basis, the wisest course is to stick to the religion one is born with, try to make the most of it, and let everyone else do the same.

One young American expressed this view very well. She once said: "I do not feel that I need to claim that Christianity is the *best* religion. It is the religion I was born into, it is my natural heritage, and I should try to live up to its ideals. As you are born with a family and a country, you are also born with a religion. You have an obligation to accept it and improve it if you can, and you should be thankful that it is there to support you if you need its support—just as your family would be there."

Exactly what a Hindu would say! In fact, the greatest Hindu of modern times, Gandhi, said this over and over. Religion is a natural inheritance, and one should accept it as he accepts citizenship in his country. But to adopt this position is to deny any religious

165

obligation to truth. All faiths are equally acceptable because there is none that is really "the way, the truth, and the life." This is to leave the last word with a kind of reverent agnosticism.

One complication ought to be looked at before we go further. Most great religions call for more or less the same kind of conduct. The same general moral principles pop up everywhere. Something like the Golden Rule can be found in nearly all scriptures. People are urged to be honest, fair, kind, patient, and peaceable. Parents are to be honored; sex life is to be orderly and faithful. All of one's more violent passions are to be restrained for the common good and the welfare of one's own soul.

Such general agreement in the moral teachings of various religions may lead one to think that their theologies are equally in agreement. The fact is, however, that ethical teachings may be based on common sense and experience as much as on theology.

The insight that "honesty is the best policy" does not necessarily depend upon a particular opinion about God. Some opinions about God may be much more effective than others in persuading one to act honestly even when it is inconvenient to do so. But the notion that honesty is desirable in general is just plain common sense. Otherwise, how could society carry on its business with any confidence and efficiency? Likewise, everyone knows what trouble the powerful emotions connected with sex can get a person into if he does not carefully discipline himself. And real lovers know that the deepest satisfactions—and even pleasures—of love do not come with random sampling but have to be developed through long and tender experience with one person.

The point is simply this: we must not assume that relative similarity in ethical principles in the various cultures means genuine similarity in the corresponding religions. Faiths with similar moral teachings may be far apart in their teaching about the meaning of the world and of human existence within it.

THE SYNCRETISTIC APPROACH

After this long wrestle with the view that all religions are really the same—equally true and equally false—we note another possible position. This would say that each religion has certain strengths and certain weaknesses, and the best thing to do is to put all these strong points together in a new faith.

In Wilmette, Ill., there stands a beautiful temple representing one such effort. Eight-sided in shape and soaring in gracefully arching lines to a lofty pinnacle, this Bahai temple represents one of approximately a hundred Bahai communities in North America. The heaviest concentration of Bahai followers is in Iran, where the movement started. A religious leader arose in 1844, proclaiming himself a prophet equal to Muhammad and announcing that an even greater Manifestation of God was about to appear. By his teaching and spiritual power, the diverse religions of mankind would be fulfilled in one universal faith. In 1850 this prophet, called the Bab (the gate) was executed and his followers savagely persecuted. In 1863, however, one of them, named Bahaullah, was accepted as the Manifestation whom the Bab had foretold. Descendants of Bahaullah have headed a world-wide Bahai movement now active in more than forty countries. The central Bahai teachings reflect the Islamic background of the movement, but with particular emphasis on the essential unity of the various religious revelations. God is unknowable except through prophetic revelations, which are continuous and progressive. All these revelations point to one evolving truth and provide a basis for unifying humanity within one faith and one way of life.

Other examples of "synthetic" religion are prominent in Japan today. The most rapidly growing groups there are a series of so-called new religions. Most of these were founded by powerful religious personalities who drew upon various elements in Japan's traditional religious culture and put them together with "new revelations" to form a distinct cult. Some of these borrow heavily from Christianity as well as Buddhism and Shinto. Whole sections of the Psalms or the New Testament are quoted in the scriptures of some sects.

Most impressive and successful of the attempts to form a new faith from the elements of earlier ones is the Sikh religion of northwest India and Pakistan. Its founder, Nanak, together with his predecessor, the great poet Kabir, consciously wove together strains from both Hinduism and Islam.

One day, after bathing in the river, Nanak disappeared in the forest and was taken in a vision to God's presence. He heard God saying: "I am with thee. I

168

have made thee happy, and also those who shall take thy name. Go and repeat Mine, and cause others to do likewise. Abide uncontaminated by the world. Practice the repetition of My name, charity, ablutions, worship, and meditation."[6] Nanak's first utterance as a prophet of the new faith was, "There is no Hindu and no Muslim."

With an Islamic emphasis upon the unity and sovereignty of God and the equality of all believers, Nanak combined typical Hindu ideas. The world is *maya* (illusion), and men live under the law of *karma* and rebirth and look to absorption in God for salvation. His disciples, known as Sikhs, grew under the leadership of ten able gurus (teachers) into a strong social and military community in northwest India. Its elite group took the name Singh (lion) and those outward marks that have identified the Sikh all over the world, the Five K's: *Kes,* long hair covered by a turban, and unshaven beard; *Kangha,* comb in the hair; *Kachk,* short drawers (the origin of khaki trousers); *Kara,* steel bracelet; and *Khanda,* steel dagger. Unfortunately, instead of reconciling Muslim and Hindu, Sikhism became simply another religion alongside its older and larger cousins.

Thus, it turned out little different from other faiths. The fact is that each religious system has drawn upon many sources. Islam arose under the influence of Jewish and Christian ideas, put together with some new elements added by Muhammad himself. Christianity sprang from Judaism, but the New Testament also shows a clear awareness of the Near Eastern mystery religions of the time. Christian theology, similarly, is heavily indebted to pagan Greek philosophers such as Plato and Aristotle. Buddhism is a stepchild of Hinduism, vastly modified and enriched in East Asia by Taoism, Tibetan polytheism, and other influences.

To live at all, a religion must continually come to terms with its environment, dealing with the main currents of thought, wrestling with practical social and moral problems, and reshaping its liturgy, architecture, and organization so as to make sense where people actually live. To this extent, the attitude is justified that we should take the finest religious ideas and convictions available, putting them together in the best possible combination.

But syncretism, the deliberate attempt to create a new and better religion out of the ideas of various faiths, is a barren strategy. Living religions are not invented in this way. They are not sewn together as a quilt is stitched out of odd-shaped pieces of cloth. Humanly speaking, they are founded only by genius and develop through centuries of living experience like a great redwood tree. No religion is simply a set of ideas. It is more like an actual landscape than a jig-saw puzzle of a landscape.

COMMITMENT PLUS THE OPEN MIND

Much more fruitful is a fourth attitude toward the faiths of men. This approach recognizes whatever values may exist in other faiths, but centers in a commitment to one's own and an eagerness to share it. Thus, I believe in God as revealed uniquely in Jesus

Christ, but I am prepared to acknowledge his working and his speaking wherever they may appear in the life of mankind. A Lutheran theologian puts it like this: "I do not establish any limits around the divine revelation, but I refuse to recognize any other God than him who reveals himself in Christ."[7]

This seems to be the viewpoint of the New Testament itself. The book of Acts reports St. Paul's address to an audience on Mars Hill in Athens. He tells his hearers that God

made from one every nation of men to live on all the face of the earth, having determined allotted periods and the boundaries of their habitation, that they should seek God, in the hope that they might feel after him and find him. Yet he is not far from each one of us, for

"In him we live and move and have our being"; as even some of your poets have said,

"For we are indeed his offspring."[8]

In other words, God made mankind one. But he also intended that men should live for long ages in distinct cultures, developed within particular areas and historical periods. Paul may have been thinking of the Egyptian culture that had sprung up in the Nile Valley five thousand years earlier and was brought to an end by Alexander the Great. Or he may have been thinking of the culture of the Tigris and Euphrates valleys of a similar period. We might add to this list the Indus River culture, ancestor of Indian civilization, or the Chinese culture that sprang up about 1500 B.C. in the great bend of the Yellow River. Each of these, suggests the apostle, was a kind of school for the human spirit in which an authentic religious quest went on "in the hope that they might feel after God and find him." Nor was God remote from them. In some real way he was present with these peoples and made his will and way felt. No wonder that there are real glimpses of truth and magnificent expressions of spiritual beauty everywhere in the panorama of man's faiths.

But there is another side to the picture. Along with insight there went deep misunderstanding. St. Paul calls it ignorance. He says that now God "commands all men everywhere to repent."[9] Clearly there is much to correct and discard in the faiths by which the various civilizations have lived. In his letter to the Romans, Paul spells out the dark side of this story:

Ever since the creation of the world his [God's] invisible nature, namely, his eternal power and deity, has been clearly perceived in the things that have been made. So they are without excuse; for although they knew God they did not honor him as God or give thanks to him, but they became futile in their thinking and their senseless minds were darkened. Claiming to be wise, they became fools, and exchanged the glory of the immortal God for images resembling mortal man or birds or animals or reptiles.[10]

Therefore, St. Paul tells the Athenians, world history has reached a turning point. Legitimate and fruitful as the religious search of all peoples has been, the whole world is now being brought under the judgment of one true faith. One single life is to become the standard for all men. One decisive revelation puts all other revelations to the test, that is, God's revelation in Jesus

172

Christ. God is going to "judge the world in righteousness by a man whom he has appointed, and of this he has given assurance to all men by raising him from the dead."[11]

This does not mean that only what is labeled Christianity will pass the test. Far from it. In fact, much that is so labeled will not pass. The Christian religion has been full of ideas and practices that are worlds away from the righteousness and faith revealed in Jesus of Nazareth. And certainly there have been saints and convictions and insights in other faiths that accord in some measure with the revelation centering in Christ. "Not every one who says to me, 'Lord, Lord,' . . . but he who does the will of my Father"[12] is accepted, said Jesus. He spoke also of those who would "come from east and west" and sit down in the kingdom of God.

In evaluating particular aspects of any religion, including Christianity, one absolutely critical question has to be answered: Is this idea, this attitude, this action in accord with the truth spoken and lived by Jesus Christ?

Steps Toward the Goal

There are three essential steps for a true Christian in encounter with other faiths. First, he must understand his own faith. He also must understand the other faiths he encounters so that he can appreciate their values as well as their defects. And he must be ready to share his own faith with others.

173

WHEN FAITH MEETS FAITH

. . . TO KNOW YOUR OWN FAITH

Understanding of one's own faith is as essential as it is rare. Most bull sessions about other religions are carried on by people who have only the haziest notion about what they themselves believe or what their own church expects them to believe. Half-baked theories about the "spiritual wisdom of the East" come very easily in such a hothouse of ignorance as the average youth group or church school class.

But there is a deeper reason for understanding one's own religion than the goal of intelligent conversation. No one has a right to call himself a Christian out of mere habit, just because he was born into a Christian family or society. This is sheer superstition. It is primitive tribal religion in the twentieth century. A person who has never faced the possibility of not being a Christian is not fully a Christian. He has never seen the demands that faith makes upon his mind and his will. He must make Christianity his own by discovering what it is and then, by deliberate decision, investing his life in those convictions and that way of life which confront us in Jesus of Nazareth. One can be a Hindu or a Shintoist or a Jew by "doing what comes naturally" in his native culture. He cannot be a Christian that way.

. . . TO UNDERSTAND OTHER FAITHS

The second stage of action to which a Christian is called as he confronts persons of other faiths is an effort to understand those faiths and to appreciate their values. You have made a beginning by reading this book. Other reading is suggested in an appendix. First-hand exploration is equally valuable. Most people to-day have opportunities to talk with Muslims, Buddhists, Hindus, and others among international students or travelers. Not only are these encounters rewarding in terms of friendship, but they can open the way to a far fuller and more sympathetic appreciation than books alone are likely to bring.

As understanding grows, one may begin to see emphases in these other faiths that can enrich his own thinking. For instance, Western religion tends to focus upon human needs and values so strongly that we forget that we share the world with other living beings. Without denying God's particular interest in mankind, nor the right of man to have dominion over the rest of creation, we need more of Buddhism's sensitivity about the wholesale torture involved in securing our daily meat supply. We might, and indeed we must, develop a far more responsible attitude toward the forests and flowers, the rivers and beaches, and the animals and birds of our planet. Someone has remarked that Americans have been given a very special gift: the power to turn everything they touch into garbage! We would move through God's world with more kindness and appreciation if we had more of Buddhism's universal compassion.

Meeting the faith of Hindus, a Christian may be challenged to rethink his own too-narrow devotion to material and moral values. In the figure of the dancing Siva, in the idea that the world is the *lila* (play) of Deity, Hinduism reminds us that existence ought to be

175

filled with enjoyment as well as effort. The Bible also speaks of the beauty of holiness and of God, but Protestant Christianity has sometimes so heavily emphasized practical service that it suggests that God is primarily a divine executive.

On another level, both Hinduism and Buddhism have conceived the world process in terms of a time span and a size more congruent with modern science than has traditional Christianity. In the theological revolution that twentieth century knowledge is stimulating, Christians may learn some lessons from the Oriental faiths about how to live religiously in a universe unthinkably vast and incredibly long lived.

Islam's tough and total commitment to the will of God may well stimulate a less mushy attitude by Christians on this point. To recognize in all that comes to us a vast divine intention that we may not understand but in which we can nevertheless rejoice by faith—this is an attitude that Muslims maintain more successfully than many Christians. An American doctor with Middle Eastern experience reports that Muslim families take death better, on the whole, than Christians. Their capacity to "accept the universe" seems to be greater. And this is surely one of the important meanings of faith in God.

None of these examples indicates that Christians may learn from other faiths truths that are totally unknown in their own tradition. But these insights are often quite buried. In the same way, one could speak of that special concern for the underdog that communism inherited from biblical faith and which it often takes far more seriously than Christians do. If nine-teenth century Christianity had not buried its treasure of social concern so thoroughly, Karl Marx and his followers might never have risen to power by the fanatical misapplication of a biblical insight.

. . . TO SHARE THE GOOD NEWS

Finally, a Christian should at all times be eager to share his faith with others. While his own living and thinking may be enriched by sympathetic encounter with other religious traditions, he should see the Good News and its communication as far more important than personal enrichment. If he really knows that Good News about God, he can no more hide it or keep it to himself than a man would light a candle and cover it with a bucket.

At a great ecumenical gathering there was considerable discussion of the question, "Why the mission of the church?" Finally, a pastor from Thailand requested the floor. "Why all this complicated argument about witnessing?" he asked. "It is simple. You witness because you must. A new baby is born; it cries. A man is reborn in Christ; he witnesses. The more the baby cries, the more you know it is a good healthy baby. The Christian is just like that."

Such sharing of the Christian faith begins, of course, with one's face-to-face encounters. All around us are persons who know little of the power that the gospel has to give life foundation and direction and zest. As we learn even a bit of what biblical faith means, we shall be eager to help others find it for themselves.

177

This may be done even more by quiet action and attitude than by words, but usually both appropriate words and effective example are necessary.

The Christian community was launched into history, however, by the great decision that its witness was not to be confined to a neighborhood or even to an entire nation, but was intended for the whole world. "You shall be my witnesses," was the mandate of the early church, "in Jerusalem and in all Judea and Samaria and to the end of the earth."[13] This reaching out to a wider encounter with men of other faiths and of no faith has usually been called missions. Today, as in New Testament times, a world mission is a necessary part of that process of sharing in which a Christian must be involved.

Through world missions, faith meets faith to the enrichment of all. The history of how the great non-Christian faiths came to be studied and understood in the Western world is vivid testimony to that. By and large it was Christian missionaries who discovered the existence and importance of these other religions. Jesuit missionaries interpreted Chinese culture to nineteenth century Europe. William Carey, pioneer of modern Protestant missions, was the first great Western student of Indian languages. All over Asia, Africa, and the Middle East, missionary scholars explored the faiths of people and passed on their findings through reports, books, and articles.

Today Christian missions still work at the never-ending task of dialogue with other faiths. At nearly a dozen centers throughout the world, the missionary

178

movement maintains small groups of specialists who devote full time to the study of the dominant religions of their area. One is located on famous Tao Feng Shan (Spirit-Wind Mountain) in Hong Kong, where for more than a generation hundreds of traveling Buddhist monks have received hospitality and joined in thought and discussion within beautiful Chinese-style buildings. Another is the Institute for the Study of Religions in Tokyo, presided over by a man who knows more about Japanese religions than any other foreigner, and perhaps as much as any Japanese does. "Operation Reach" is the name given to a program of Islamic studies carried on by a greatly gifted Anglican priest whose books on Islam are among the best in English.

The results of such work are passed on through conferences, interviews, conversations, and reading, to the church around the world. So understanding grows.

Christian Commitment Creates Change

In another way, Christian missions carry forward the process of sharing. For over a century they have been stimulating other faiths to re-examine themselves under the challenge of Christian values and convictions. Sometimes the imitation of Christian organizational forms is a tip-off: the Y.M.H.A. (Young Men's Hebrew Association) or Y.M.B.A. (Young Men's Buddhist Association); the development of Sunday schools by Jews and Buddhists; and such a children's song as "Buddha loves me, this I know!"

More significant are deep transformations within

other faiths as they confront the standard represented in Jesus Christ. Muslims have been telling the story of their great Prophet for thirteen centuries. In recent generations the way of telling it has shifted considerably. Modern biographies of Muhammad emphasize his humility, self-sacrifice, self-restraint, peaceableness. They minimize other characteristics that used to be prominent in the tradition: his military prowess, his extensive relations with women. One gets the distinct impression that the Man of the gospels has had something to do with shaping this twentieth century image of Islam's greatest man.

Again, in modern Buddhism the old negative concepts are being reinterpreted very much in the spirit of the Christian faith. *Metta* (world-embracing love) is expounded as a principle of social action. Mere good will and benevolent thoughts are now to be completed by outgoing service to mankind. *Anatta,* traditionally the denial of any enduring self, now means only that self-love and egoism are to be combatted; it does not deny the existence and the importance of the individual person. In nirvana, positive aspects are stressed instead of the "blowing-out" so important in the beginning. Its blessedness, its positive happiness and peace resemble very much what Christianity has described as eternal life.[14]

Building Spiritual Foundations

Another major contribution of Christian missions today stems from their ministry to people, especially young people, caught in a religious vacuum due to the breakdown of their ancestral faiths. A distinguished American scholar who spent several months teaching in Japan wrote: "No Christian can come as close to the minds of young Orientals as I was privileged to come . . . without a deep sense of compassion for their stunned, confused, disoriented frame of mind."[15] Faith cannot, of course, be handed over in such a situation as if it were an overcoat. Nevertheless, the need is there. In a world where the acids of modern thought and feeling have everywhere eaten away the beliefs and morals of people, Christians are called to testify as honestly and vividly as they can to a real and saving faith.

Whole societies also need this Christian help in finding a spiritual basis for life in our puzzling and dangerous world. The distinguished Yale philosopher, F. S. C. Northrop, has pointed out one reason why Christian missions are needed today as never before: non-Western peoples are demanding higher standards of living, which can only come with scientific technology. But this technology requires large capital expenditure, which in turn calls for financial integrity and use of the Western law of contract, and these rest upon the ethics and religion of the West. "Thus the economic problem in Asia is at bottom an ethical, legal, and religious problem, which involves the understanding of Western law, ethics and religion for its effective solution."[16]

Above all, the problem of our age is that of building an international society in which war waged with H-bombs, bacteriological weapons, and other highly civilized horrors will become impossible. Such a society must be, in fact, a single world culture with the same kind of unity as the tribal and national cultures of the past have had in limited areas. But in all history, there is no example of a society finding stability and unity without being anchored in a common faith. Every enduring and creative community has had a religious core. It is altogether likely that this will be true also of the coming world civilization.

What will this spiritual foundation for a world of human brotherhood be? We have scanned the faiths of mankind and have examined their concerns and their convictions. Now we must decide, as the world must decide, where it is that such a universal faith foundation may be found. Do we not find a clue in some familiar words of the New Testament?

"The God and Father of our Lord Jesus Christ . . . destined us in love to be his sons through Jesus Christ, according to the purpose of his will, . . . set forth in Christ as a plan for the fullness of time, to *unite all things in him,* things in heaven and things on earth. . . . For he is our peace."[17]

This is the claim with which the Christian faith meets the other faiths of men. It does not claim that it has all truth and that they are all error. Nor does it assert that Christians and their church are perfect, or necessarily better than men of other religions. The Christian claim is that the God who made all men of one blood is working to bring them into one brotherhood, reconciled with one another and with himself. And that the story of Jesus Christ, told in words and expressed in deeds by the fellowship of his followers, has God's own power in it and will some day bring the age-old divine plan to fulfillment.

Such a statement is more than a witness and much more than a claim. It is, in addition, a condemnation of all forms of Christianity that do not reconcile men to one another and to God. And it is a challenge to all Christians to get on with their mission in a world that cannot and will not wait forever to hear and to see this gospel.

NOTES

CHAPTER 1. All Men Seek God

1. *Time*, December 20, 1940. Quoted in Roger L. Shinn, *Beyond This Darkness* (New York: Association Press, 1946), p. 13.
2. Freud develops such a line of thought in *The Future of an Illusion* (Institute of Psychoanalysis, 1928).
3. Cf. Heinrich Zimmer, *Philosophies of India* (New York: Pantheon Books, Bollingen Series XXVI, 1951), p. 279.

CHAPTER 2. Hinduism

1. Based on Swami Nikhilananda's *Hinduism: Its Meaning for the Liberation of the Spirit* (New York: Harper & Brothers, 1958), pp. 53f.
2. Cf. Stuart Pigott, *Pre-historic India* (Harmondsworth, Middlesex, England: Penguin Books, 1950), pp. 202f.
3. Reuters, Ltd., August 1, 1955.
4. *Times of India Directory*, Bombay, 1961-62.
5. *Life*, February 7, 1955.
6. S. Radhakrishnan, *Eastern Religions and Western Thought* (London: Oxford University Press), pp. 20ff.
7. *Occasional Bulletin* (New York: Missionary Research Library), May 27, 1958, p. 7.
8. *Bhagavad-Gita*, trans. Swami Prabhavananda and Christopher Isherwood (New York: Mentor Books, 1954 [by permission of Marcel Rodd, orig. publisher]), pp. 38ff.
9. C. F. Andrews, *Mahatma Gandhi's Ideas* (London: George Allen and Unwin, Ltd., 1929), p. 129.
10. *Bhagavad-Gita*, pp. 38ff.
11. C. F. Andrews, *op. cit.*, p. 129.
12. *Bhagavad-Gita*, p. 37.

13. *Ibid.*, pp. 37f.
14. Malcolm Pitt, *Introducing Hinduism* (New York: Friend-ship Press, 1955), p. 11.
15. Heinrich Zimmer, *Philosophies of India* (New York: Pantheon Books, Bollingen Series, XXVI, 1951), p. 11.
16. Nikhilananda, *op. cit.*, p. 45.
17. Pitt, *op. cit.*, p. 36.
18. Nikhilananda, *op. cit.*, p. 184.
19. Pitt, *op. cit.*, p. 31.
20. *Bhagavad-Gita*, p. 49.
21. Nikhilananda, *op. cit.*, p. 124.
22. *Ibid.*, pp. 128-143.
23. *Ibid.*, pp. 162f.
24. *Life*, February 7, 1955.
25. Based on Andrews, *op. cit.*
26. J. C. Winslow, *The Christian Approach to the Hindu* (London: Edinburgh House Press, 1958), p. 32.
27. T. S. Avirashilingam, *Understanding Basic Education* (1955), p. 1.
28. Andrews, *op. cit.*, p. 192.

CHAPTER 3. Buddhism

1. Based on S. W. Holmes, "The Significance and Value of Zen to Me," *Religion in Life*, Summer, 1959.
2. Clarence H. Hamilton, *Buddhism* (New York: The Liberal Arts Press, 1952), p. 17.
3. *Ibid.*, p. 22 (modified).
4. E. A. Burtt, *The Teachings of the Compassionate Buddha* (New York: Mentor Books, 1955), p. 35.
5. *Ibid.*, pp. 34-35.
6. *Ibid.*, p. 30.
7. There is also a Buddhist list of "Ten Immoral Actions": killing, stealing, unchastity, lying, slandering, harsh languages, frivolous talk, covetousness, ill will, and false views.
8. Kenneth W. Morgan, *The Path of the Buddha* (New York: The Ronald Press Company, 1956), p. 112.
9. *Life*, March 7, 1955, p. 81.
10. J. B. Pratt, *The Pilgrimage of Buddhism* (New York: The Macmillan Company, 1928), p. 22.

NOTES

11. Paul Elmer More, *The Sceptical Approach to Religion* (Princeton, The Princeton University Press, 1934), p. 23.
12. Pratt, *op. cit.*, pp. 4 and 9.
13. Burtt, *op. cit.*, p. 60.
14. Pratt, *op. cit.*, p. 98. Cf. Morgan, *op. cit.*, pp. 3, 73, 75.
15. *Ibid.*, p. 54.

CHAPTER 4. Watershed of Religions

1. John B. Noss, *Man's Religions* (New York: The Macmillan Company, 1956), p. 385.
2. Jer. 18:6.
3. Gen. 12:1-3.
4. Isa. 5:16.
5. Hos. 2:19f; 11:1-5 (selected).
6. Gen. 1:26.
7. Psa. 104:24, 27, 29, 30.
8. Amos 5:24.
9. Micah 6:8.

CHAPTER 5. Judaism

1. Deut. 6:4-5.
2. Deut. 6:6-7.
3. Deut. 12:23.
4. Deut. 14:6, 8.
5. Deut. 14:21.
6. Deut. 16:1.
7. Deut. 16:18.
8. Deut. 22:1.
9. Deut. 22:5.
10. Deut. 23:20.
11. Deut. 24:5.
12. Deut. 6:8.
13. TV panel on Judaism, Ch. 2, Boston, August 20, 1961.
14. Milton Steinberg, *Basic Judaism* (New York: Harcourt, Brace and Company, 1947), p. 36.
15. *Commentary*, April, 1961.
16. Martin Buber, *I and Thou* (Edinburgh: T & T. Clark, and New York: Charles Scribner's Sons, 1937, trans. by R. G. Smith), pp. 79, 95.

CHAPTER 6. Christianity

1. Mark 1:15.
2. Luke 6:27-31.
3. Luke 10:30 ff.
4. Acts 2:38f.
5. Isa. 53:4-5.
6. Rom. 5:1.
7. Matt. 28:18-20.
8. 1 Cor. 11:24f.
9. This is the title of a popular Roman Catholic tract.

CHAPTER 7. Islam

1. Sura 96. This and other quotations from the Koran are from *The Meaning of the Glorious Koran:* An Explanatory Translation by Muhammad Marmaduke Pickthall (New York: Mentor Books, 1953).
2. Sura 4.
3. Sura 2.
4. Sura 50.
5. Sura 24.
6. Sura 17.
7. Sura 6.
8. Sura 56.
9. Sura 35.
10. Based on Sura 45.
11. Sura 2.
12. See, for example, Suras 2 and 5.
13. Kenneth W. Morgan, *Islam: The Straight Path* (New York: The Ronald Press Company, 1958), p. 171f.
14. *Ibid.*, p. 175.

CHAPTER 8. Communism

1. Karl Marx, *Capital*, Modern Library Giant Series (New York: Random House, 1932), p. 513f.
2. Karl Marx, *The Communist Manifesto.*
3. *Ibid.*
4. *The Selected Works of Mao Tse-tung* (London: Lawrence, Lawrence and Wishert Ltd., 1954-56), III, pp. 849-880.
5. *Quarterly Notes*, Christian Study Centre on Chinese Religion (Shatin, N.T., Hong Kong: Tao Fong Shan), March, 1961.

NOTES

6. Based on an actual document, quoted from *Measure of a Moment,* by Helen Kromer.
7. George Orwell, *1984* (New York: Harcourt, Brace and Company, 1949), p. 267.
8. *Ibid.,* p. 271.
9. R. C. Crossman, ed., *The God That Failed* (New York: Harper & Brothers, 1950).

CHAPTER 9.   The Distinctiveness of My Own Faith
1. John Dewey, *A Common Faith* (New Haven: Yale University Press, 1934), p. 87.
2. Rom. 8:38 f.

CHAPTER 10.   Called to Witness
1. Reported in the *New York Herald Tribune,* April 5, 1959.
2. *Chicago Daily News,* May 18, 1960, p. 25.
3. W. E. Hocking, *The Coming World Civilization* (New York: Harper & Brothers, 1956), p. 149.
4. Ewbank of the Baltimore Colts, reported in *New York Times* News Service. Former President Eisenhower and others have said much the same thing.
5. *Southeast Asia Journal of Theology,* July, 1961, p. 40.
6. John B. Noss, *Man's Religions* (Revised Edition; New York: The Macmillan Company, 1956), p. 278.
7. Gustaf Aulén, in a lecture at Union Theological Seminary, New York, 1947.
8. Acts 17:26-28.
9. Acts 17:30.
10. Rom. 1:20-23.
11. Acts 17:31.
12. Matt. 7:21.
13. Acts 1:8.
14. *Southeast Asia Journal of Theology,* July, 1961.
15. Horton, Walter Marshall, Ms. of an address, February, 1961.
16. Northrop, F. S. C., "Comparative Religion in Today's World," in *The Christian Century,* Sept. 14, 1955, p. 1051.
17. Eph. 1-2.

FOR FURTHER READING

Only a few of the many available books on man's religious faiths can be listed here. Readers seeking further information are referred to encyclopedias and to card catalogues in public libraries for additional titles and to their own church headquarters for denominational literature in this field.

GENERAL TREATMENTS

Appleton, George, *Glad Encounter* (London: Edinburgh House, 1959). A presentation of the Christian faith, setting forth Jesus Christ as the One with whom men of all religions may have a "glad encounter."

Cooke, Gerald, *As Christians Face Rival Religions* (New York: Association Press, 1962). A sensitive approach to the new religious situation, in which faiths confront each other more fully.

Neill, Stephen, *Christian Faith and Other Faiths: The Christian Dialogue with Other Religions* (London: Oxford University Press, 1961). A substantial survey and theological analysis by a leading ecumenical thinker.

Noss, John B., *Man's Religions* (Third Edition; New York: Macmillan and Company, 1963). A thorough textbook, well organized and clearly written.

TREATMENTS OF SPECIFIC RELIGIONS

Hinduism

Pitt, Malcolm, *Introducing Hinduism* (New York: Friendship Press, 1955). Vividly written by a Western authority on India and its foremost religion.

FOR FURTHER READING

Winslow, Jack C., *The Christian Approach to the Hindu* (London: Edinburgh House, 1958). Helpful for Christians who seek to understand Hinduism as well as to Hindus who confront the challenge of Christian faith.

Buddhism

Appleton, George, *On the Eightfold Path: Christian Presence Amid Buddhism* (New York: Oxford University Press, 1961). An attempt to discover what Buddhism means to the Buddhist as well as what are the essentials of the Christian approach.

Latourette, Kenneth Scott, *Introducing Buddhism* (New York: Friendship Press, 1956). A compact, popular survey of Buddhism by a renowned scholar.

Judaism

Gordis, Robert, *The Root and the Branch: Judaism and the Free Society* (Chicago: University of Chicago Press, 1962). An authoritative explanation of Judaism for the Christian reader.

Steinberg, Milton, *Basic Judaism* (New York: Harcourt Brace and Company, 1947). A lucid presentation of the Jewish religion, written from within.

Christianity

ROMAN CATHOLIC

Adam, Karl, *The Spirit of Catholicism* (New York: Macmillan Company, 1941). A presentation of the Roman Catholic position concerning the church.

Pelikan, Jaroslav, *The Riddle of Roman Catholicism* (New York and Nashville: Abingdon Press, 1959). An evaluation by a Protestant student of Roman Catholicism.

EASTERN ORTHODOX

Benz, Ernst, *The Eastern Orthodox Church* (New York: Doubleday Anchor, 1963). A comprehensive and competent treatment of the history, spirit, and beliefs of Orthodoxy.

FOR FURTHER READING

Meyendorff, John, *The Orthodox Church* (New York: Pantheon Books, 1962). A thorough treatment of the faith and history of this branch of Christendom by one of its priests.

PROTESTANT

Brown, Robert McAfee, *The Spirit of Protestantism* (New York: Oxford University Press, 1961). A presentation of Protestant convictions, well written and very readable.

Dillenberger, John and Welch, Claude, *Protestant Christianity* (New York: Charles Scribner's Sons, 1955). A competent analysis from the historical perspective.

Islam

Cragg, Kenneth, *Sandals at the Mosque: Christian Presence Amid Islam* (New York: Oxford University Press, 1959). A sympathetic presentation, by an Anglican clergyman who understands Islam thoroughly, of the Christian approach to Muslims today.

Wilson, J. Christy, *Introducing Islam* (Revised Edition; New York: Friendship Press, 1958). A brief and readable treatment of Islam and the Christian approach to it.

Communism

Bennett, John C., *Christianity and Communism Today* (New York: Association Press, 1960). A readable guide, by a careful scholar, to the complex problems of modern Communism and Christianity's stance in relation to it.

Wilson, Frank Price, *Marx Meets Christ* (Philadelphia: Westminster Press, 1957). Through a comparison of Christianity and Communism on several levels, offers provocative insights into the nature of both.

A WORD ABOUT THE FORMAT

Type: Linotype Primer, 10 point leaded 3 points
Composition, press, and binding:
Sowers Printing Company, Lebanon, Pa.
Covers: Affiliated Lithographers, Inc., New York, N. Y.
Typographic Design: Margery W. Smith